T0214723

Communications in Computer and Information Science 1372

More information about this series at http://www.springer.com/series/7899

Prafulla Kumar Behera ·
Purna Chandra Sethi (Eds.)

Digital Democracy – IT for Change

53rd Annual Convention
of the Computer Society of India, CSI 2020
Bhubaneswar, India, January 16–18, 2020
Revised Selected Papers

Springer

Editors
Prafulla Kumar Behera 🆔
Utkal University
Bhubaneswar, India

Purna Chandra Sethi 🆔
Rama Devi Women's University
Bhubaneswar, India

ISSN 1865-0929   ISSN 1865-0937   (electronic)
Communications in Computer and Information Science
ISBN 978-981-16-2722-4   ISBN 978-981-16-2723-1   (eBook)
https://doi.org/10.1007/978-981-16-2723-1

This Springer imprint is published by the registered company Springer Nature Singapore Pte Ltd.
The registered company address is: 152 Beach Road, #21-01/04 Gateway East, Singapore 189721, Singapore

Preface

The development of technology for digital democracy has brought about better implementation and monitoring of government programs. Digital platforms over the years have built a bridge of communication between the government and the citizens. These platforms have massive potential for deeper and broader public participation along with the capacity to rebuild and strengthen democratic institutions and the relationship between stakeholders.

The main purpose of technology is to bring information and comfort while keeping a check on its judicious use. We promote technology and harness its potential for social good but when human life and values become inferior it can bring about destruction and fear. The world has now become a global village with digital connectivity, which can be further developed into a family with the inclusion of human values, equality and justice. The Computer Society of India has an important role to play in this process with events like CSI 2020, which help integrate technology for good governance and to elicit grassroots participation.

CSI 2020 was held in Bhubaneswar, India, during January 16–18, 2020, with the theme of "Digital Democracy - IT for Change". This Communications in Computer and Information Science (CCIS) Volume 1372 disseminates the proceedings via eleven informative chapters. The conference focused on four major areas: digital democracy, digital communication, digital analytics, and digital security; these tracks were chaired by Prof. Manas Ranjan Patra, Prof. Siba Kumar Udgata, Prof. Annappa B., and Prof. Durga Prasad Mohapatra, respectively. Digital democracy involves the use of Information and Communication Technology (ICT) in political and governance processes. Digital communication deals with effective online communication. Digital analytics focuses on efficiency as well as the optimization process. Lastly, digital security deals with the security aspects of digital communication so that loss of data can be minimized and data security can be achieved during communication.

The conference would not have been possible without the valuable support and guidance of the General Chair, Prof. Lalit Mohan Patnaik (Adjunct Professor and INSA Senior Scientist, National Institute of Advanced Studies, India). We are very grateful for the participation of all speakers in making this conference a memorable event.

We are highly confident that readers will get useful information pertaining to digital democracy from this contribution. We would like to convey our sincere thanks to all the authors who have contributed the papers in the eleven chapters of this book along with their priceless time and efforts.

April 2021

Prafulla Kumar Behera
Purna Chandra Sethi

Organization

General Chair

Lalit Mohan Patnaik National Institute of Advanced Studies, India

Program Chair

Prafulla Kumar Behera Utkal University, India

Track Chairs

Manas Ranjan Patra Berhampur University, India
Siba Kumar Udgata University of Hyderabad, India
Annappa B. NIT, Karnataka, India
Durga Prasad Mohapatra NIT, Rourkela, India

Convener

Purna Chandra Sethi Rama Devi Women's University, India

Reviewers

Salman Abdul Moiz University of Hyderabad, India
Arup Abhinna Acharya KIIT University, Bhubaneswar, India
S. Anuradha GITAM University, Visakhapatnam, India
Purushothama B. R. NIT, Goa, India
Shambhavi B. R. BMS College of Engineering, India
Bikash Ranjan Bag Berhampur University, India
Sambit Bakshi NIT, Rourkela, India
Rakesh Balabantaray IIIT, Bhubaneswar, India
Soubhagya Sankar VIT, Amerabati, India
   Barpanda
Basavaraju IBM, Bengaluru, India
Sabita Behera CIME, Bhubaneswar, India
Nagappa Bhajantri Sri Jayachamarajendra College of Engineering, India
Sourav Bhoi PMEC, India
Poongodi Chinnasamy Vivekanandha College of Engineering for Women,
   India
Aravinda C. V. NMAM Institute of Technology, India
Demian Antony D'Mello Canara Engineering College, India
Ranjita Das NIT, Mizoram, India
Abhimanyu Dash OUAT, India

Ranjan Kumar Dash	CET, India
Ratnakar Dash	NIT, Rourkela, India
Shatarupa Dash	SOA University, India
Ramesh Dharavath	IIT (ISM) Dhanbad, India
Rahul Dixit	IIT (ISM) Dhanbad, India
Chandralekha	Utkal University, India
Poornalatha G.	NIT, Karnataka, India
Ramesh Chandra G.	VNR Vignana Jyothi Institute of Engineering and Technology, India
Umashankar Ghugar	Berhampur University, India
Aghila Gnanasekaran	NIT, Puducherry, India
Geetha J.	Ramaiah Institute of Technology, India
Om Prakash Jena	Ravenshaw University, India
Prema K.V.	Manipal Institute of Technology, India
Umamaheswar Achari Kakinada	Charter Communications, USA
Bonomali Khuntia	Berhampur University, India
Saraswati Koppad	NIT, Karnataka, India
Anand Kumar M.	NIT, Karnataka, India
Manoj Kumar M V.	NIT, Karnataka, India
Madhu Kumar S. D.	NIT, Calicut, India
Shipra Kumari	National Institute of Fashion Technology, India
Shyam Lal	NIT, Karnataka, India
Anupkumar M. Bongale	Symbiosis Institute of Technology, India
Dhiraj M. Dhane	IIT, Kharagpur, India
Judhistir Mahapatro	NIT, Rourkela, India
Roshan Martis	Vivekananda College of Engineering and Technology, India
Venkatesan Meenakshi Sundaram	NIT, Karnataka, India
S. Mini	NIT, Goa, India
Brojo Kishore Mishra	GIET University, India
M. Mishra	SOA University, India
Sambit Kumar Mishra	SOA University, India
Sonali Mishra	SOA University, India
Dipak Misra	XIMB, India
Namita Mittal	MNIT, India
Jnyanaranjan Mohanty	KIIT University, India
Jyoti Ranjan Mohanty	OUAT, India
Sanjukta Mohanty	NOU, India
Sujata Mohanty	NIT, Rourkela, India
Susil Kumar Mohanty	University of Hyderabad, India
Debasis Mohapatra	Berhampur University, India
Ramesh Kumar Mohapatra	NIT, Rourkela, India
Seli Mohapatra	C.V. Raman Institute of Technology, Bhubaneswar, India

Lalatendu Muduli	Bhadrak College, India
Ruchira Naskar	IIEST, Shibpur, India
Ajit Kumar Nayak	SOA University, India
Biswojit Nayak	Utkal University, India
Padmalaya Nayak	Gokaraju Rangaraju Institute of Engineering Technology, India
Samaleswari Prasad Nayak	SIT, Bhubaneswar, India
Sradhanjali Nayak	NIIS, Bhubaneswar, India
Abdul Nazeer	NIT, Calicut, India
Antony P. J.	A J Institute of Engineering and Technology, India
Venugopala P. S.	NMAM Institute of Technology, India
Srurthi P.	TCS, Ernakulum, India
Sudarsan Padhy	SIT, Bhubaneswar, India
Mrutyunjaya Panda	Utkal University, India
Manisha Panda	Berhampur University, India
Sanjaya Kumar Panda	NIT, Warangal, India
Subhrakanta Panda	BITS Pilani, India
Ashalata Panigrahi	Berhampur University, India
Vikas Panthi	NIT, Rourkela, India
Marcin Paprzycki	Polish Academy of Sciences, Poland
Anjaneyulu Pasala	IIITDM, Kurnool, India
Annapurna Patil	MSRIT, Bengaluru, India
K. Sridhar Patnaik	BIT Mesra, India
Rasmi Ranjan Patra	OUAT, India
Binod Kumar Pattanayak	SOA University, India
Prasant Kumar Pattnaik	KIIT University, India
Pandaba Pradhan	BJB Autonomous College, India
Sateesh Kumar Pradhan	Utkal University, India
Krishna Prakasha	MIT, India
Shubha Puthran	NMIMS, India
Vinayakumar R.	Jegga Research Lab, USA
Satya Champati Rai	SIT, Bhubaneswar, India
Vijay Rajpurohit	KLS Gogte Institute of Technology, India
Satyajit Rath	IMMT, India
Bnb Ray	Utkal University, India
Mitrabinda Ray	NIT, Rourkela, India
Damodar Reddy Edla	NIT, Goa, India
Raghavendra S.	Shri Madhwa Vadiraja Institute of Technology and Management, India
Samrat Sabat	University of Hyderabad, India
Ajit Sahoo	University of Hyderabad, India
Biswapratap Singh Sahoo	NTU, Taiwan
Pulak Sahoo	SIT, Bhubaneswar, India
Ramesh Sahoo	IGIT Sarang, India
Bharat Jyoti Ranjan Sahu	SOA University, India

Swamynathan Sankara Narayanan	Anna University, India
Sanjeev Sannakki	KLS Gogte Institute of Technology, India
Korra Sathya Babu	NIT, Rourkela, India
Purna Chandra Sethi	Rama Devi Women's University, India
Srinivas Sethi	IGIT Sarang, India
Suraj Sharma	IIIT, Bhubaneswar, India
Jagannath Singh	KIIT University, India
Kavita Singh	Yeshwantrao Chavan College of Engineering, India
Adepu Sridhar	Singapore University of Technology and Design, Singapore
Ranjita Swain	NIT, Rourkela, India
Santosh Swain	KIIT University, India
Satya Swain	Bharat Electronics, Bangalore, India
Satyabrata Swain	NIT, Rourkela, India
Likewin Thomas	PESITM, India
Deepak Tosh	University of Texas at El Paso, USA
Alok Ranjan Tripathy	Ravenshaw University, India
Hrudaya Kumar Tripathy	KIIT University, India
Pradyumna Kumar Tripathy	SIT, Bhubaneswar, India
Vasudeva	NIT Karnataka, India
Srinivasa Murthy Y. V.	NIT, Karnataka, India

Contents

Decentralized Voting System Using Block Chain Technology

Rupali Deshmukh[✉], Olivia Biswas[✉], Servina Bardeskar[✉],
and Harshavardhan Lad[✉]

Fr. Conceicao Rodrigues Institute of Technology, Vashi, Navi Mumbai 400703,
Maharashtra, India

Abstract. Voting is an integral part of any organization which helps organizations to take important decisions after taking a consensus from others and help implement any idea/decision in a procedural manner. But current voting methods like ballot box and digital voting systems face a lot of security threats like DDoS attacks, fake votes, alteration and manipulation of votes, malware attacks, etc. This creates a sense of mistrust amongst the traditional voting systems. In proposed system, use of blockchain technology to minimize the flaws of existing system and make voting process more secure, reliable, and transparent. To resolve the issues in current existing voting system this paper suggests use of Blockchain Technology for enhancing security and decentralization of data.

Keywords: Blockchain · Decentralized · Security · Voting

1 Introduction

1.1 Existing System

Traditional voting systems like Ballot based voting have been around in the history of the voting process for quite some time [1]. The Kudavolai system used in village assembly elections in Tamil Nadu, around 920 AD can be considered as an example first use of ballots for voting. But the scenario took a different course during the 1990s where cases of ballot stealing, fake/bogus paper votes, booth capturing, etc. where reported, eventually leading to its downfall. The early 1990s saw the rise of electronic and digital voting systems which offered enhancements in security, labor work and integrity. These devices were made to prevent fraud by putting a limit on how fast new votes can be entered into the electronic machine and are currently used in many countries for their election processes. The first country to deploy electronic voting system for elections was Estonia which was soon followed by countries like Switzerland and Norway for their state and council elections respectively [2]. An e-voting system should be highly secured so that not only it's available to voters but also overcomes the challenges faced by current voting systems like tampering with the voter's ballot or changing votes. Many electronic voting systems currently claim to offer anonymity of voters by using Tor network but fail to hide voter identity as intelligence agencies often spy on the Internet

© Springer Nature Singapore Pte Ltd. 2021
P. K. Behera and P. C. Sethi (Eds.): CSI 2020, CCIS 1372, pp. 1–11, 2021.
https://doi.org/10.1007/978-981-16-2723-1_1

and identify voters or intercept their votes. There were many flaws like malicious software programming, susceptibility to fraud, accuracy in capturing voter's intent, vulnerability to hacking, political ties of manufacturers, secure storage of cast votes, etc. Because of this, electronic voting devices and electronic voting was not taken into practice on a global scale. Moreover, many of the countries (including the Netherlands, Great Britain, Germany), where e-voting was initially widespread, ultimately limited its use due to the imperfection of the technology and they returned to the more reliable method of voting [3]. With such monumental decisions at stake and the development of technology and society both pushing to search for cheaper and more reliable methods of voting, the need for a secure, automated, transparent and automated voting system comes into picture. This paper aims to pertain the methodology to automate, digitalize, and decentralize the current voting systems by using block chain technology so as to remove the flaws in the current existing system (Table 1).

1.2 Blockchain Technology

Blockchain is a collection of distributed ledger technologies that can be programmed to record and track anything of a value. It is simple a chain of blocks, kind of database that stores digital information. The term 'Blockchain' was first coined by Satoshi Nakamoto (pseudonym) [4], who presented the idea of a peer to-peer system that allowed users to make digital payments by transacting cash through the Internet without the involvement of any middleman. Each block on a blockchain is cryptographically linked to the previous block i.e. the foundation of the stack is the first block in the chain. The previous block gets layered one after the other each new block created to form a stack called a Blockchain.

Information in blockchain is stored in a shared and continually reconciled database. The information isn't stored in any single location, hence it is public and easily verifiable. Ledger technology is a centuries old non- destructive way to track data changes over time. It could be financial transactions, medical records or even votes. Blockchain Technology helps to simplify the system as following

1. **Tamperproof**
   In a blockchain, each block is connected cryptographically to its previous block with the help of special technique called Hashing. Hence, if any change is attempted on the block values, it is immediately reflected in the hash of previous block, giving an alert. Therefore, once data is inserted, it cannot be rewritten and makes the block tamperproof.
2. **Decentralized**
   Centralization means power in only handful of people/database. They monetize data and have access to all personal data.The decentralized nature means that no central authority has the power to handle the blocks. It is only with the help of consensus of other nodes that blocks are added into the chain after a rigorous process of validation. This reduces the chance of corruptness in the procedure. To maintain cryptography Hashing and encryption decentralized ledger is used by the block chain. As there is no central authority we can assure that the monitoring of the third party is prohibited and access to the database is limited. System failure is in control in the decentralized system.

Table 1. Comparitive study on various system.

Sr. no	Paper title	Description	Advantages	Disadvantages
1	Overview of the emerging technology: Blockchain [14]	Blockchain types like Colored coins-dealing with assets, Hyperledger, Ethereum, etc. explained. Cryptographic principles used. Use of digital signatures	Secure, block added only after verification	Broadcasting takes time
2	Electronic voting machine—A review [11]	Electronic Voting Machine (EVM) is a simple electronic device used to record votes in place of ballot papers and boxes which were used earlier in conventional voting system	Eliminates human errors, easier to use, time saving, secure than paper ballot voting	Hardware and software not safe, Vulnerability to hacking, tampering of casted votes
3	Design of Distributed Voting Systems [12]	A detailed study on various voting systems around the world, highlighting the merits and demerits of each system. (Estonian iVoting system, Norwegian I-Voting System, New South Wales iVote System)	Cryptography used, public and private keys, secure, encrypted	Centralized infrastructure, Dedicated servers, but all in one data center, multiple voting, hacking, DDos attacks, Lack of security personnel
4	Bronco Vote: Secure Voting System using Ethereum's Blockchain [15]	BroncoVote implements a university-scaled voting framework that utilizes Ethereum's blockchain and smart contracts to achieve voter administration and auditable voting records. In addition, BroncoVote utilizes a few cryptographic techniques, including homomorphic encryption, to promote voter privacy. Using MetaMask and Web3 eliminates the need for users to download full or even partial Ethereum blockchains on their local machines in order to broadcast transactions	Transparent, secure, cost effective	Support for cryptography limited, Computational power is slow
5	Blockchain Based E-Voting System Design [16]	Evaluates blockchain frameworks, blockchain technology can be one solution to solve the problems that often occur in the electoral system. The use of hash values in recording the voting results of each polling station linked to each other makes this recording system more secure and the use of digital signatures makes the system more reliable	Resistance to Failures, Invulnerability to Network Censorship, Users are More Likely to Trust an Application that is Not Controlled by One Governing Body	Difficulty of Development, Applications Need to Verify The Identity of The User, Robustness of Network for Dedicated Purposes

3. **Trust**

   The block is created so that the cryptographic puzzle must be solved. Secondly, the computer that solves the puzzle, shares the solution to all the other computers on the network. This is called proof of work [5]. The network will then verify this proof of work, and if verified is then added to the network. The combination of these complex math puzzles and verification by so many computers, ensures that only a genuine block is added.

4. **No intermediaries**

   No middlemen involved between transactions who are hired or approached, to view someone's records and keep it confidential. But, here, the user himself can prove his ledger's Genuity by himself and hence this peer-to-peer interaction with data allows cutting out cost and middlemen involved.

2   Voting System

The first step in the process is to take information from the user and validate and automate the process by identifying legitimate users. After users are verified voters can cast their vote but their identity remains anonymous. After each vote is verified only then the vote is added into the block,otherwise it is discarded [6]. All the transaction get started with the timestamps to increase transparency. Lastly,real time result are shown and upload, also no vote can be manipulated since no central authority has control on it. The following are the steps describing how the proposal works.

2.1   Login

The voter puts in his credentials for logging into the system - in this case it would be using a 12 digit voter ID that is issued during registration, fingerprint and a onetime password(OTP) that is sent by the system to the voter's mobile at the time of login. If the credentials provided are correct, the user is allowed to go to next page otherwise access is denied.

2.2   Cast Vote

Voters now come across the voting page that has all the details of the candidates taking part in the election, the user has to select any one candidate. User is prompted to confirm his voting as voting can be done only once. All this is done through a user friendly website.

2.3 Encrypting Votes

As the user chooses the candidate, it's time to covert to encrypt everything and convert it into a fixed length hash as our aim is to fasten the process of voting by converting variable length data that includes Voter Id, Voter account address, his credentials, vote that he has casted, etc. to a fixed length hash value for faster processing. This uses SHA one way hashing technique that cannot be reversed and is send for verification.

SHA stands for Secure Hashing Algorithm. On getting a certain set of input characters, this algorithm converts variable length input strings/integers into fixed size characters called Hash. It generates unique value for a given input and the generated function is of fixed size 256 bits (32 bytes) [7]. If an attacker attempts to retrieve voter information, he has to perform a brute force attack of guessing thousands of hash combinations that give back the voter account value, which is practically impossible. Hence encryption makes the process secure.

2.4 Adding Vote to Blockchain

Using protocols like consensus and proof-of-work, a block is added into the chain after validation.

3 System Design

(See Fig. 1).

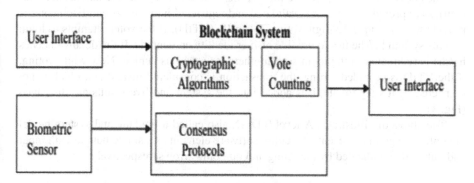

Fig. 1. Architectural block diagram of voting system

The above block diagram depicts the interaction between the three modules of the system. The inputs from User Interface module (Website) consists of user credentials, registration and login details whereas the Biometric Sensor being the hardware interface provides the fingerprint of the voter. Inputs from both the modules interact with the Blockchain system that encrypts, verifies and validates the votes and provides a secure channel for the voting process. The results are then displayed on the User Interface (Fig. 2).

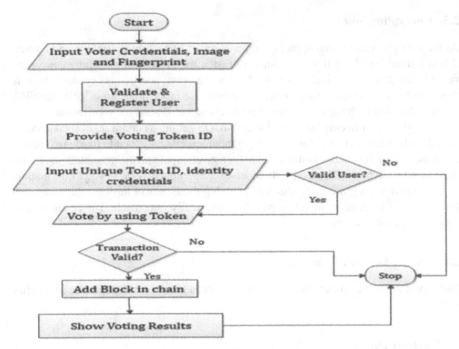

Fig. 2. Flowchart of the voting system

The above diagram depicts the flow of the system. After voter credentials and bio-metrics are provided, the user is validated and registered into the system. Each voter is provide with a unique 12 digit Voting Token ID (VTID). If the voter attempts to login into the system he/she has to provide his/her identity credentials. If the details matches he/she is redirected to the login screen otherwise access is denied. Now while voting, if the VTID is provided wrong, the transaction is considered invalid and block is not registered. If it's legitimate, it is added into the system and live results are displayed (Fig. 3).

The above dig illustrates A level 0 DFD, also called a fundamental system model or context diagram represents the entire software element as a single bubble with input and output data indicated by incoming and outgoing arrows, respectively.

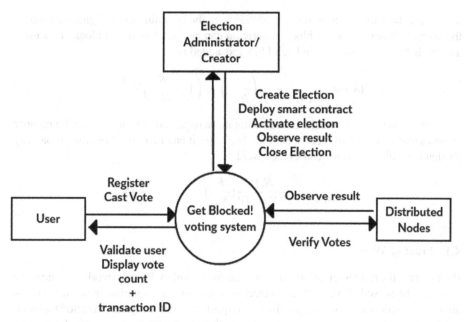

Fig. 3. DFD level1 system design

4 Algorithms Used in Block Chain

Algorithm in block chain are used for the modification and validation of blocks. Consensus algorithm is widely used for the validation in block chain [4]. This algorithm further can be identified into Proof of work algorithm and Proof of Stake algorithm. Consensus algorithm is mainly used when there is any faulty or non-working node. It ensures that the information is transferred to all the nodes and blocks present. Single data value among distributed processes or systems is used to achieve agreement by Consensus algorithm process. Multiple unreliable nodes are involved to. With the help of consensus algorithm, we can reach out to every node. Which will help us to identify that the block added to the system is successful or not.

It is the inbuilt algorithm which keeps audit of all the blocks present. This helps the system to work without interrupt and flawlessly. Each and every block is audited as soon as the transaction takes place. Updating of blocks is also done by this algorithm. It prevents system failure due to any faulty block addition to the system. Each and every node is monitored as it gets newly add to the system. here due to this redundancy is reduced and every node is checked. Consensus also helps to prevent different types of attack like dos attack. As every block is added only after verification this makes to identify attack. Solving the issue, known as the consensus problem, is important in distributed computing and multi-agent systems. When node generates and transfers the data and consensus problem arises then BFT helps to overcome and make sure that the information in system is safe if issue occurs then liveliness occurs within $[(n-1) \div 3]$, n is the number of replication occurs nodes can be handled up to 33%. 3F + 1 faulty node can be handled. [7] Using the consensus algorithm N/2 + 1signature should be present to become the valid block into the system, where the N is number of signature send by the commissioner [8]. Valid block generation can be called as round block consensus. The probability that we can find valid block is added is-

$$P(X) = \frac{N_c!}{X!(N_c - X)!}\left(\frac{K}{N_{bc}}\right) \times \left(1 - \frac{K}{N_{bc}}\right)N_c - X \qquad (1)$$

In order to make the results of the voting more impartial, it is hoped that the number of votes that a butler can receive exceeds Nc/2. So, it can be figured out the probability P1 that a candidate's votes can exceed Nc/2

$$P1 = \sum_{i=N_c/2}^{N_c} \frac{N_c!}{i!(N_c - i)!}\left(\frac{K}{N_{bc}}\right)^i \times (1 - \frac{K}{N_{bc}})N_c - i \qquad (2)$$

4.1 Proof of Work

Poof work is the implementation of the consensus algorithm. Proof of work is the mystery that is to be solved if we find the correct way to solve the solution is not far. This is analogous to a solve the mystery. Effort are required to put the mystery solution together, but it takes only a momentary solution to see that if one has been concurred correctly. In Proof of Work consensus, the effort required to solve a mystery is called Work, and a solution is called a Proof of Work [9]. In other words, the solution to the mystery proves that someone did the work to find that solution. Blockchains which use Proof of Work algorithm consensus require exact proof to create new block and added to the blockchain. This is used to add new blocks into block chain. This Work is frequently referred to as 'mining.'

5 Results

- Creation of blockchain account for storing the vote and user details.
- Creating the blockchain contracts for maintaining authenticity, and securing information.
- Sending of Ether to other accounts for validation of vote, successful addition of vote.

The screenshot of implemented modules is shown below (Figs. 4, 5 and 6):

Fig. 4. Blockchain token for vote transfer

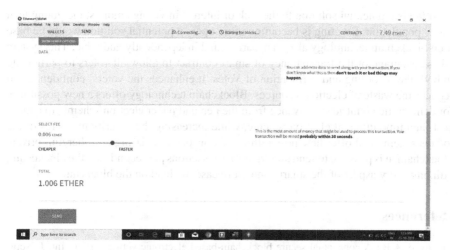

Fig. 5. Ether added to the account.

Fig. 6. Account showing number of total ether present

6 Conclusion

E-voting is a potential solution to the lack of interest in voting amongst the young tech savvy population. E-voting is becoming more open, a potential solution would be base it on blockchain technology also transparent, and independently auditable. This system takes advantage of the transparency of smart contract to allow all voters to participate in both the recording and verification of Votes. It enhances the voters' confidence and reduces the waste of election resources. Blockchain technology offers a new possibility for democratic countries to advance from the pen and paper election scheme, to a more cost- and time-efficient election scheme, while increasing the security measures of the todays scheme and offer new possibilities of transparency. Using an Ethereum private blockchain, it is possible to send hundreds of transactions per second onto the blockchain, utilizing every aspect of the smart contract to ease the load on the blockchain.

References

1. Ayed, A.B.: A conceptual secure blockchain-based electronic voting system. Int. J. Netw. Secur. Appl. **9**(3), 1–9 (2017). https://doi.org/10.5121/ijnsa.2017.9301
2. Meter, C., Schneider, A., Mauve, M.: Tor is not enough: coercion in remote electronic voting systems. arXiv preprint (2017)
3. Bach, L.M., Mihaljevic, B.: Comparative analysis of blockchain consensus algorithms. In: 41st International Convention on Information and Communication Technology, Electronics and Microelectronics (MIPRO) (2018)
4. Li, K., Li, H., Hou, H., Li, K., Chen, Y.: Proof of vote: a high-performance consensus protocol based on vote mechanism consortium blockchain. In: IEEE 19th International Conference on High Performance Computing and Communications; IEEE 15th International Conference on Smart City; IEEE 3rd International Conference on Data Science and Systems (HPCC/SmartCity/DSS) (2017)

5. Yavuz, E., KaanKoc, A.: Towards secure e-voting using Ethereum blockchain. In: International Symposium on Digital Forensic and Security (ISDFS), at Antalya, Turkey, vol. 6 (2018)
6. Hardwick, F.S., Gioulis, A., Naeem, R.: E-Voting with Blockchain: An E-Voting Protocol with Decentralisation and Voter Privacy (2018)
7. Hanifatunnisa, R., Rahardjo, B.: Blockchain based e-voting recording system design. In: 11th International Conference on Telecommunication Systems Services and Applications (TSSA) (2017)
8. Gerlach, J., Grasser, U.: Three Case Studies from Switzerland: E-voting. Berkman Center Research Publication (2009)
9. Brakeville, S., Bhargav, P.: 18 March 2018. https://developer.ibm.com/tutorials/cl-blockchain-basics-intro-bluemix-trs/
10. https://en.wikipedia.org/wiki/Electronic_voting_in_India#Voter-rifiable_paper_audit_trail
11. Ashok Kumar, D., Ummal Sariba Begum, T.: Electronic voting machine – a review. In: International Conference on Pattern Recognition, Informatics and Medical Engineering (PRIME-2012), TamilNadu (2012)
12. Springall, D., Finkenauer, T., Durumeric, Z.: Design of Distributed Voting Systems, 24 September 2015. https://arxiv.org/pdf/1702.02566.pdf
13. Barnes, A., Brake, C., Perry, T.: Digital Voting with the use of Blockchain Technology (2016). https://www.economist.com/sites/default/files/plymouth.pdf
14. Chatterjee, R., Chatterjee, R.: An overview of the emerging technology: blockchain. In: International Conference on Computational Intelligence and Networks, Bhubaneswar, India (2017)
15. Dagher, G.G., Marella, P.B.: BroncoVote: secure voting system using Ethereum's blockchain. In: 4th International Conference on Information Systems Security and Privacy (ICISSP), San Francisco (2018)
16. Hjálmarsson, F.Þ.: Blockchain-based e-voting system. In: IEEE 11th International Conference on Cloud Computing (2018)

Factors Affecting Programming Skill of the Students – An Exploratory Analysis

Sherna Mohan[✉] and E. R. Vimina[✉]

Department of Computer Science and IT, Amrita Vishwa Vidyapeetham,
Kochi Campus, Kochi, India

Abstract. One of the issue encountered in computer programming courses are the high failure rate among the students. This is a serious concern for educators and the students. So there is a dire need to diagnose the factors affecting the same. Hence the objective of this study is to analyse the programming skill of the students by considering the factors like educational background, program debugging skill etc. Methods like correlation and regression are adopted for analysing these factors. It is observed that the debugging skill of the student has an upper hand in determining the programming skill compared to the marks secured in the examinations.

Keywords: Programming skill · Performance · Behavior · Correlation · Debugging · Regression

1 Introduction

There is a high failure rate and drop outs occurring in the computer programming courses. Students are often finding difficulty in programming. So educators have to take extra effort in identifying the weak students and device proper strategy to improve their programming performance. In this study certain factors are investigated which are obligatory for the programming skills of the students. Hitherto major studies focused on the demographics [2], educational background [4], prior programming experience [6], mathematical ability of the students in the examination [3, 7] etc. are used to predict the programming skill.

In computer programming papers, students are given various programming assignments which are expected to be completed within a stipulated time period. The evaluation of these assignments helps the educators to identify the programming skills of the students. Hence the objective of the proposed work is to explore the factors that can be used to determine the programming skills of the students. In order to predict the programming behavior, some methods are used for recognizing the hidden relationship among the attributes of the dataset. The following factors are considered for the analysis.

- Marks obtained in the qualifying examination, especially the marks scored in mathematics [3, 7].
- Programming behavior of the student for the given assignment which is analysed through debugging capability.

© Springer Nature Singapore Pte Ltd. 2021
P. K. Behera and P. C. Sethi (Eds.): CSI 2020, CCIS 1372, pp. 12–18, 2021.
https://doi.org/10.1007/978-981-16-2723-1_2

This paper is organized as follows. The background work is described in Sect. 2 and proposed approach in Sect. 3. In Sect. 4, results and discussions are analysed and finally, in Sect. 5 the conclusions and future scope are explained.

2 Related Works

Over the past decades, several researchers have been attempting to study the academic performance of the students by analysing the factors which affect the programming behavior of the students. So there are various data mining techniques can be used to predict students programming performance. In [1] relationship between the gender and the marks obtained in the final examination by the students are analysed using chi square test and it is observed that there is no significant relationship between the same. They used deep learning methodology to predict the grade of the students. Another study [2] deals with prediction of students' performance in final examination using the linear regression and multilayer perceptron in WEKA tool and compared the greatness between the mean absolute error value differences. Based on the 58 participants from Taiwan University [3], the study predict the academic performance using students final grades to improve learning performance with the help of multiple linear regression and principal component analysis.

Sujatha [4] predict student performance with the help of regression algorithms and found risky students who need more attention in the programming based on the features of higher secondary school background details, the medium of study, syllabus covered, marks scored in mathematics and English etc. Based on the data points collected from different undergraduate courses [5], a new set of multivariate linear regression model is used to predict the final exam score in the Engineering dynamics course. The data mining technology aids to assess the learner's performance and help us to implement various new trends and technologies to analyse the data [6]. Another paper [7] statistically found that there is no correlation between the performance of computer subjects in high school and the performance in the first year programming course.

3 Proposed Approach

The objective of the investigation is to analyse the programming skills of the students by considering the factors like marks obtained in the qualifying examination, debugging skill etc. So the weaker students can be identified in advance and the educator can help them to improve their programming skills. In the present scenario, while analysing the factors affecting the programming skills of the student, we consider:

- The marks secured in the qualifying examination especially the marks obtained in the mathematics subject [3, 7].
- The programming behavior of the student by analysing the debugging capability of a student.

The dataset for this study is prepared by collecting the details of first year computer science students. The details of 108 students were collected, out of which 35 were males and 73 were females. The chosen students were from different educational backgrounds. Programming questions and the difficulty levels (Easy (E), Medium (M) and Hard (H)) were prepared by the educators. For the dataset preparation, the programming assignments were allotted to the students based on the first year curriculum programming language. The teacher indistinguishably distributed programming assignments to each students and finally collect the debugging outputs of each student.

Programming outputs were analysed based on the number of errors in each compilation, number of errors occurred in the penultimate compilation, number of compilation attempts etc. Various types of errors like syntax errors, semantic errors were also identified during the analysis process. While debugging a program, students may attempt multiple compilations to arrive at the final output. The maximum number of errors occurred and penultimate compilation error values are recorded during the compilation process. This way we reach the debugging capability of the students in three levels (E, M and H) and the numerical values should be normalized within the range from 0 to 1. The compilation attempts and errors occurred during the debugging stage are used to quantify the debugging capability. The formula for calculating debugging capability is given as

$$DC_{std1} = 1 - \left(\frac{PCE_{max} - PCE_{min}}{CA} \right) \tag{1}$$

Where

- DC_{std1} = Debugging capability of individual student
- PCE_{max} = maximum number of errors occurred while debugging a single program in the compilation
- PCE_{min} = number of errors occurred in the penultimate compilation while debugging a single program in the compilation
- CA = Total number of compilation attempts made by the student to reach the programming output.

3.1 Methodology

As discussed in the introduction, the primary goal of this study is to investigate the factors which influence the programming skills of the students by considering the marks obtained in the qualifying examinations and programming behavior of the students. Better programming practices not only solves the programming problem but also expand their coding creativity. Pearson correlation and Regression methods are adopted for analysing the factors. 70% data were considered as training set and remaining set as testing data.

Factors Influencing the Programming Skill

Here we find the correlation analysis of marks obtained by the students in various examinations and analysing the programming behavior using linear regression methodology.

In order to figure out the dependence between various potential factors we first correlate the final marks and mathematics marks secured in qualifying examination with final marks obtained in the examination of the current programming course. The criterion variable used for this research was the marks obtained in the final examination of the programming course. Pearson correlation coefficient is the statistical correlation method used in this study and it was calculated as

$$r = \frac{n(\sum xy) - (\sum x)(\sum y)}{\sqrt{[n\sum x^2 - (\sum x)^2][n\sum y^2 - (\sum y)^2]}} \tag{2}$$

In the above correlation method, n is the number of students, x and y determines the marks obtained in qualifying examination and in the final examination. By definition, the coefficient of correlation assumes any values in the interval between -1 and $+1$. The statistical correlation values between the above attributes shown in Table 1 and the Fig. 1 shows the correlation between the marks obtained in the qualifying examination and the marks secured in the final examination. It is pointed out that programming behavior of a student is weakly correlated with marks secured in the qualifying examination.

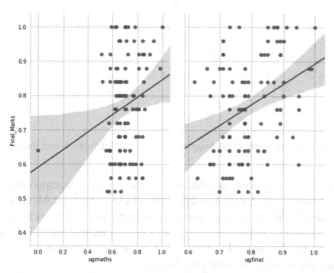

Fig. 1. Correlation between the qualifying marks and final marks

Next, for analysing the programming behavior of the students, we correlate debugging skill and the final marks obtained in the examination of the current programming course. The debugging capability is used for predicting the programming behavior of the students and the quantified value of debugging capability can be computed using the Eq. (1) which is prescribed in Sect. 3. Linear Regression method is used for analysing the programming behavior which indicates the strength of the impact between multiple independent variables and a dependent variable. The linear regression prediction result was displayed as below:

$$Y = 0.405 - 0.011 * DC_E + 0.465 * DC_M + 0.11 * DC_H \tag{3}$$

Where DC_E, DC_M and DC_H deals with debugging capability of each student in different levels (Easy, Medium, Hard) and the computation is shown in Eq. (1). Here the response variable (dependent variable) used in this study is final marks secured in the examination of the current programming course. Figure 2 shows the strong positive correlation between the marks obtained in the final examination and the debugging capability of students in different levels (Easy, Medium and Hard). From this, it is pointed out that debugging skill of the student has an upper hand in determining the programming skill compared to the marks secured in the examination.

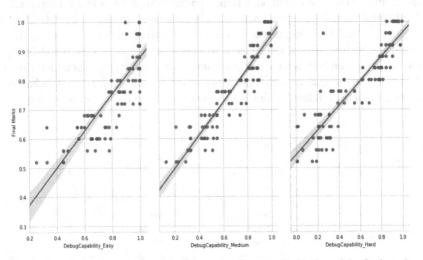

Fig. 2. Correlation between the debugging capability of each levels and the final marks

Furthermore, the study needs an evaluation metric in order to compare the predictions with the actual values. So, Mean Absolute Error (MAE) and Root Mean Square Error (RMSE) are the two common prediction error measurement methods used for finding the score of the continuous variables. They are used to measure the difference between values predicted by the regression model and the values actual observed. MAE and RMSE are calculated using the following formulas:

$$MAE = \frac{1}{n} \sum_{j=1}^{n} \left| y_j - y_j' \right| \tag{4}$$

$$RMSE = \sqrt{\frac{1}{n} \sum_{j=1}^{n} \left(y_j - y_j' \right)^2} \tag{5}$$

Here y_j and y_j' are the attributes specified in the above discussion. R^2 and MSE measures can evaluate the goodness of fit of a regression model. The accuracy of prediction is measured by the standard error of the estimate. By comparing Fig. 2 with Fig. 1, the values are very closer to the regression line which minimizes the sum of squares error. Therefore by minimizing the sum of squared deviations of prediction, the predictions in Fig. 2 is more accurate than Fig. 1. The R^2, mean absolute error, mean squared error and root mean squared error values were shown in Table 2.

Table 1. Results obtained by the correlation analysis

Performance Criteria	Marks obtained for Mathematics in qualifying examination	Final Marks secured in qualifying examination	Debugging capability (Easy Level)	Debugging capability (Medium Level)	Debugging capability (Hard Level)
Final marks secured in the examination	0.21	0.35	0.83	0.92	0.89

4 Results and Discussion

In this segment, we will discuss the results of factors influencing the programming skill of the students using correlation and regression. From Table 1, it is observed that the marks obtained in qualifying examination (especially mathematics marks and final marks 0.21 and 0.35) are positively correlated with final marks obtained in the current programming course. Also it is observed that there is a strong positive correlation between the debugging capability of the student (0.83, 0.92, and 0.89) with the final marks. By considering the regression model, R^2 value is 0.81 and evaluation metric values MAE and RMSE have very less residual values (from Table 2) which produces better prediction. From Fig. 2, it is analysed that regression line minimizes the sum of squared errors. So more accurate the prediction. From the above analysis it can be predicted that programming behavior is strongly correlated with final marks in the examination than marks obtained in the qualifying examination. This will aid the educators to learn more about the weak students and identify better techniques to impart programming skills to those students.

Table 2. The results of linear regression model

Feature affecting the programming skill	Coefficient of Determination	Mean Absolute Error (MAE)	Mean Squared Error (MSE)	Root Mean Squared Error (RMSE)
Debugging Capability	0.81	0.047	0.0033	0.218

5 Conclusion and Future Study

Apart from predicting the programming skills, the presented work represents the exploratory analysis of the factors which affect the programming behavior of the students. It is observed that debugging skill of a student is highly correlated with final marks obtained in the examination of the current programming course. So it is concluded that debugging skill of the student has an upper hand in determining the programming skill compared to the marks secured in the examinations. Therefore as a future work, by considering the programming behavior of the current situation, we plan to carry out a similar study covering more number of potential success factors to improve the performance of the students in programming.

References

1. Pal, V.K., Bhatt, K.K.V.: Performance prediction for post graduate students using artificial neural network. Proc. Int. J. Innov. Technol. Explor. Eng. **8** (2019)
2. Widyahastuti, F., Tjhin, V.U.: Predicting students performance in final examination using linear regression and multilayer perceptron. In: 2017 10th International Conference on Human System Interactions (HSI), pp. 188–192. IEEE (2017). https://doi.org/10.1109/HSI.2017.8005026
3. Yang, S.J., Lu, O.H., Huang, A.Y., Huang, J.C., Ogata, H., Lin, A.J.: Predicting students' academic performance using multiple linear regression and principal component analysis. J. Inf. Process. 170–176 (2018). https://doi.org/10.2197/ipsjjip.26.170
4. Sujatha, G., Sindhu, S., Savaridassan, P.: Predicting students performance using personalized analytics. Int. J. Pure Appl. Math. 229–238 (2018). https://www.ijpam.eu
5. Huang, S., Fang, N.: AC 2010-190: regression models of predicting student academic performance in an engineering dynamics course. In: American Society for Engineering Education (2010)
6. Sagar, M., Gupta, A., Kaushal, R.: Performance prediction and behavioral analysis of student programming ability. In: 2016 International Conference on Advances in Computing, Communications and Informatics (ICACCI), pp. 1039–1045. IEEE (2016). https://doi.org/10.1109/ICACCI.2016.7732181
7. Ayalew, Y., Tshukudu, E., Lefoane, M.: Factors affecting programming performance of first year students at a university in Botswana. Afr. J. Res. Math. Sci. Technol. Educ. **22**(3), 363–373 (2018). https://doi.org/10.1080/18117295.2018.1540169

A Study of Agile Iterative Development Methodology on Web Application Quality

Rayaguru Akshaya Kumar Das$^{(\boxtimes)}$ and A. B. Khan

Institute of Management and Information Technology, Cuttack, Cuttack, Odisha, India

Abstract. With the increase in use of web based applications in different fields, the competition for providing secure efficient and quality software increases with a demand for decreased cost of the product. To improve the product development process in environment of the ever dynamic customer requirement and to meet the quality parameters of the software products many in the industry, have adopted agile software development. Although the nuances of agile methods like iterative development existed decades back the term Agile software development was coined in 2001 in a small group industry meet. In this paper we have tried to scan the literature for any correlation between the agile development methods and software quality. We have conducted a survey to understand how one of the major factors of agile development i.e. iterative development influences the quality of the software.

Keywords: Agile development · Iterative methods · Web application · Software quality · Web application quality

1 Introduction

The modern software applications, irrespective of size and sophistication and size are driven by quality motive. Quality motive is a prime driving force in modern software industry. The customers want value of their money in terms of quality. The quality of software applications, especially important in the present scenario where almost all the applications are web based and are very complex, multi-tired, sophisticated. This forces some core changes to the traditional software development method. Agile software development method is considered to be one such solution to gain advantage in this cutthroat competition age. After that many of the industry leaders have adopted the Agile development method for better quality products [13, 14]. In this paper, we will try to establish some known parameters of agile development to the software quality of service based web applications.

2 Literature Review

Even though the software industry has comprehensively understood and embraced the agile methods, not much empirical study has been done to examine the agility parameters

P. K. Behera and P. C. Sethi (Eds.): CSI 2020, CCIS 1372, pp. 19–26, 2021.
https://doi.org/10.1007/978-981-16-2723-1_3

and its effect on quality of the software products [7–11]. Most of the studies are based on the productivity and performance of the software application.

Consequently, there are many studies covering iterative or incremental software development and software productivity. Behem [2] measures productivity as output to input of the process. Some of the drivers of the productivity are volatility of the requirement, use of different modern tools, program complexity etc. Krishnan [3] in an imperial study tried to find correlation between productivity and quality which is expressed as product size, use of tools quality and capability of the development team etc. Behrens [4] discussed the way to apply different function points to the productivity measurement. The productivity trends in software iterative development are outlined by Thomas [5]. He tried to find out the relationship between the different attributes of productive trends like stability of staffing, adaptability of design to the iterative development. Claudia de O et al. [12] conducted a case study on productivity and suggested that the software companies need to reorganize the organizational structure and find out the best fit between the organizational structure and agile methodology. Bohem et al. [13] suggested a method and strategy for incremental application development and tradeoff of strategies. Shetal S [15] suggested that the factors which affect the quality of the software are reliability usability reusability extensibility portability etc. Two scholars Li & Calantone conducted empirical study on 236 software professionals to determine the relationships between customer market knowledge, competence and performance. Beck, Jiang, & Klein surveyed 286 software personnel involved in development to determine the effects of prototyping on project performance. What they found was prototyping use, learning, and interactions were correlated to project success.

Separate studies were also carried out for web site web portal quality. Yang and others [16] conducted empirical study involving 1,992 web users to determine the relationships between service quality and overall quality of Internet portals. They conclude that the usability, usefulness, adequacy, accessibility, and interaction of Internet portals were correlated to their overall quality. Two scholars Sullivan & Walstrom surveyed 82 designers to formulate instrument to measure website quality. Tsikriktsis conducted a study on 171 web users and found that an instrument measuring website quality was correlated to cultural dimensions. Many such similar studies were undertaken by different scholars. However, we are unable to find a single study which tries to co-relate the iterative development of Agile development to website quality. We are unable to find a single study where the iterative deployment is directly compared to the software quality.

3   Software Quality

There are many quality models for software. Some of the quality models are: Mc Calls's model, Boehms Model, FURPS model, Ghezzi Model, IEEE model, Dromey's model, Stac's model, CMM (Capability Maturity model), EtailQ model etc. For our research we have chosen the "EtailQ" model which is very much suitable for e-commerce websites and other service oriented websites. Presently most of the websites and the underneath web application provides some kind of service. Hence we feel that the EtailQ model is one of the appropriate models to measure the quality of web applications. The parameters measuring the website quality in the EtailQ model are: Fulfillment and reliability, Privacy and security, Website design and customer service. The EtailQ model gives an instrument to measure the parameters. For our research, we interpreted each of the parameters of quality in the following manner (Table 1):

Table 1. Web site quality parameters

Quality parameter	Measurable variable
Fulfillment and reliability	Received order
	Delivery time
	Accuracy of order
Website design	In-depth information
	Efficiency of order processing
	Processing speed
	Product selection
	Personalization
Privacy and security	Feeling of safety
	Protection of safety
	Adequate security
Customer service	Willingness to respond to customer need
	Willingness to fix the issues
	Proficiency in answering the customer queries

For our study we have used the above mentioned parameters to measure the quality of the web portal. As it is evident from the above table the by measuring three parameters we can measure fulfillment and reliability which is just one of the four components of quality.

4 Agile Software Development Methodologies

The Quest for quality software and the short duration for the software development lead to more and more software development firms moving from traditional software development methodologies to Agile software development methodology. The characteristic feature of the Agile software development methodology are better customer interaction, shorter development cycle, frequent design changes to accommodate the customer feedback and incremental product delivery. The Agile development is driven by the Agile manifesto [20]. There appeared several version of agile development like Extreme programming (EX), Scrum, Kanban etc with some variation in different parameters. In spite of the difference, all the above mentioned methodologies have some basic common parameters. One of the common parameter which is common to all the agile development methodologies such as XP, Scrum and Kanban is iterative development. One of the main thrusts of Extreme Programming is continuous and effective interaction with the customer so that the customer feedback is incorporated in the software as soon as possible, thereby changing the previous version of the software. The main driving force of such iterative development of software is based on the customer feedback. The Scrum development also talks about iterations. In Scrum, the iterations are called sprints. For the entire duration of the sprint extensive planning is needed. At the end of each sprint, a check is carried out to find possibility of areas positional improvement to the product. The Kanban methodology of Agile software development recommends the use of short iterations. Thus in the modern software or web application development, iteration plays an important role as the competition and the ever dynamic world requires the software to be dynamic and capable of accommodation the changes quickly effectively without compromising the software quality.

5 Iterative Development

According to Larman, iterative development as a software development method which is defined as "an approach to building software (or anything) in which the overall lifecycle is composed of several iterations in sequence". Furthermore, "each iteration is a self-contained mini-project composed of activities such as requirements analysis, design, programming, and testing." Iterative development is a lifecycle of software development. The iterative development is generally used to evolve operational software into finished products gradually. This is done by continuously and constantly incorporating customer feedback, test results and other problems discovered into its design. Iterative development falls under the category of time-boxed design, meaning that delivery dates are fixed by reducing product requirements. In simpler term, iterative development refers to a much more dynamic release of beta versions using the Internet. Different scholars have used different sub-factors for iterative development. There are different ways of quantifying the iterative development. However, for our study, we will consider the following five sub-factors of iterative development. These are:

(a) Time-boxed releases: software release based on time
(b) Operational releases: software release based on operation or increment
(c) Small releases: software release based on small iterations
(d) Frequent releases: software release like in weekly monthly etc.
(e) Numerous releases: software release in multiple increments.

6 Objective

The goal and the objective of the study are very clear and precise. The objective of the research was to find out if there is any correlation between the Agile iterative development to the website quality. The iterative development of agile development is becoming popular among the developers. This may imply a strong reason that the iterative development causes better quality products. This assumption has to be formulated in form of hypothesis and proved to confirm the assumption. The hypothesis was formulated as:

Hypothesis - (H1): "Implementation of Iterative development methodology corresponds to produces quality web-application"

It is not straightforward to measure the quality of web-application. The EtailQ quality model has four sub-factors namely website design, website privacy and security, website reliability and customer service. Hence, we somehow need to quantify the different parameters of web-application quality with the iterative development method. The effect of the iterative development on website design, privacy and security, reliability and need fulfillment and customer service need to be established. Considering the sub factors of the website quality, it would be logical and to suggest four sub– hypothesis. The suggested sub-hypothesis are:

Hypothesis 1a - (H1a): Implementation of Iterative development methodology corresponds to better web-application designing capability
Hypothesis 1b - (H1b): Implementation of Iterative development methodology ensures privacy and security.
Hypothesis 1c - (H1c): Implementation of Iterative development methodology corresponds to higher reliability and customer need fulfillment.
Hypothesis 1d - (H1d): Implementation of Iterative development methodology corresponds to better customer service.

The justification for formulation of hypothesis and sub-hypothesis that the quality is complex and is associated with different aspects. Due to its complexity the hypothesis is broken down to the sub-hypothesis there by making somehow easy to do an empirical study to ascertain the quality. Broadly, quality requirements are "characteristics that make the product attractive, usable, fast or reliable" [23]. In order to incorporate the feedback of one particular quality parameter the next product might compromise the other quality aspects. Hence all the quality parameters has to be measured against each version launched after iterative development.

7 Data Analysis

Data collected from the software professionals developing web applications in the agile iteration based development and they are asked to name the sites which uses the web applications in the full stack. Another independent assessment was done to evaluate the quality of the web application by interacting with the sites which uses the web applications. For our study the survey instruments will consist of a five point Likert-type scale from with numerical values from one to five. The lowest being score 1 and the highest is considered to be score 5. As per the plan, data were collected for software design methods, website quality, and project outcomes. Almost 1506 respondents responded to the questionnaire on different web application design methods, and 324 respondents responded on web application quality data. Correlation analysis was conducted on the above parameters and are displayed in Table 2. Pearson correlation was conducted and the values of adjusted R^2 values are is calculated. After that there is the need to reduce the data for easy analysis. In the next step the website quality data is examined. Like in the previous case the Pearson correlation analysis were performed on the 14 variables of website quality and the result is prepared and analyzed. On analysis it is found that many of the variables associated with each of the four major parameters of website quality were found to be closely correlated.

Table 2. Correlation analysis of iterative development

Factor	1	2	3	4	5	Respondents	score
Time-boxed releases	135 (9%)	195 (13%)	75 (5%)	451 (30%)	646 (43%)	1502	3.85/5 (77%)
Operational releases	60 (4%)	136 (9%)	241 (16%)	361 (24%)	708 (47%)	1506	4.01/5 (80.2%)
Small releases	90 (6%)	135 (9%)	284 (19%)	404 (27%)	583 (39%)	1496	3.84/5 (76.8%)
Frequent releases	134 (9%)	223 (15%)	208 (14%)	402 (27%)	521 (35%)	1488	3.64/5 (72.8%)
Numerous releases	90 (6%)	285 (19%)	315 (21%)	270 (18%)	540 (36%)	1500	3.59/5 (71.8%)

Adjusted R2 values of the data based on the website quality is analyzed and it is found that almost all the groups have high adjusted R2 values. This was especially true for the last two groups i.e. Fulfillment and reliability and customer service. This analysis implies that the variables are correlated within individual categories and the website quality instrument is reliable and valid.

Based on the data a statistical model is prepared. The four major factors of web application quality are represented in which columns to the rows figuring the iterative development in Table 3.

Table 3. Web-application quality factor analysis

Factor	Variable	Website design	Privacy and security	Fulfillment and reliability	Customer Service	Composite
Iterative development	*Adjusted R^2 value*	0.546	0.860	−0.120	−0.187	0.326
	F-value	3.163	12.053	0.807	0.716	1.872
	Significance	*0.144*	0.016	*0.599*	*0.644*	*0.282*

Five statistical models were constructed between the four major factors of website quality (including a composite model called eTailQ) and iterative development. The model, privacy and security and fulfillment and reliability as a function of iterative development have high adjusted R^2 value and are statistically significant. The composite quality model was significant at the 0.10 level, which was far above the minimum threshold for significance used in this analysis.

8 Conclusion

Based on the data analysis of the hypotheses and sub-hypotheses was performed. There was some evidence that iterative development was correlated to website quality, website design, privacy and security, and fulfillment and reliability at the 0.05 level. The summary is presents in the Table 4.

Table 4. Model analysis

	Hypothesis	β	t-value	p-value
Iterative development	H1 Iterative development → Website quality	0.758	0.039	$p < 0.05$
	H1a Iterative development → Website design	0.745	0.028	$p < 0.05$
	H1b Iterative development → Privacy and security	1.029	0.007	$p < 0.05$
	H1c Iterative development → Fulfillment and reliability	0.634	0.040	$p < 0.05$
	H1d Iterative development → Customer service	0.632	*0.286*	$p > 0.10$

From this it is clear that the hypothesis H_{1a}, H_{1b}, H_{1c} are accepted and the hypothesis H_{1d} may not be accepted as it is outside the threshold of significance. The Main hypothesis H1 is accepted. Thus we came to the conclusion that the agile iterative development increases the web application quality.

References

1. Rodríguez-Hernández, V., et al.: Assessing quality in software development: an agile methodology approach. J. Adv. Comput. Sci. Technol. **4**(2), 225–230 (2015)
2. Boehm, B.W.: Improve software productivity. Computer **20**(9), 43–57 (1987)
3. Krishnan, M.S., Kriebel, C.H., Kekre, S., Mukhopadhyay, T.: An empirical analysis of productivity and quality in software products. Manag. Sci. **26**(6), 745–759 (2000)
4. Behrens, C.A.: Measuring the productivity of computer systems development activities with function points. IEEE Trans. Softw. Eng. **9**(6), 648–652 (1983)
5. Tan, T., Li, Q., Boehm, B., Yang, Y., He, M., Moazeni, R.: Productivity trends in incremental and iterative software development. In: Proceedings of 3rd International Symposium on Empirical Software Engineering and Measurement, ESEM 2009, pp. 1–10. IEEE Computer Society, Washington, DC (2009)
6. Lee, G., Xia, W.: Toward agile: an integrated analysis of quantitative and qualitative field data. MIS Q. **34**(1), 87–114 (2010)

7. Sudhakar, G.P., Farooq, A., Patnaik, S.: Soft factors affecting the performance of software development teams. Team Perform. Manag. **17**, 187–205 (2011)
8. Balijepally, V., Mahapatra, R., Nerur, S.P., Price, K.H.: Are two heads better than one for software development? The productivity paradox of pair programming. MIS Q. **33**(1), 91–118 (2009)
9. Dybå, T., Arisholm, E., Sjøberg, D.I.K., Hannay, J.E., Shull, F.: Are two heads better than one? On the effectiveness of pair programming. IEEE Softw. **24**, 12–15 (2007)
10. Shull, F., Melnik, G., Turhan, B., Layman, L., Diep, M., Erdogmus, H.: What do we know about test-driven development? IEEE Softw. **27**, 16–19 (2010)
11. de Melo, C.D.O., Cruzes, D.S., Kon, F., Conradi, R.: Interpretative case studies on agile team productivity and management. Inf. Softw. Technol. **55**(2), 412–427 (2013)
12. Oberscheven, F.M.: Software quality assessment in an agile environment. Faculty of Science of Radboud University in Nijmegen (2013)
13. Khalane, T., Tanner, M.: Software quality assurance in Scrum: the need for concrete guidance on SQA strategies in meeting user expectations. In: 2013 International Conference on Adaptive Science and Technology (ICAST). IEEE (2013)
14. Sheetal, S., Sarkar, D., Gupta, D.: Agile processes and methodologies: a conceptual study. Int. J. Comput. Sci. Eng. **4**(5), 892 (2012)
15. Yang, H., Cao, J.: B2E Portal Integration Conceptual Architecture Framework, Economics and Management School, North University of China
16. Wolfinbarger, M., Gilly, M.C.: eTailQ: dimensionalizing, measuring and predicting etail quality. J. Retail. **79**(3), 183–198 (2003)
17. Li, Y.N., Tan, K.C., Xie, M.: Measuring web based service quality. Total Qual. Manag. **13**(5), 685–700 (2002)
18. Tsikriktsis, N.: Does culture influence web site quality expectations? An empirical study. J. Serv. Res. **5**(2), 101–112 (2002)
19. Wolfinbarger, M., Gilly, M.C.: Etailq: dimensionalizing, measuring, and predicting etail quality. J. Retail. **79**(3), 183–198 (2003)
20. Agile Manefisto. https://agilemanifesto.org/principles.html
21. Awad, M.A.: A comparison between agile and traditional software development methodologies. University of Western Australia (2005)
22. Sharma, M.K.: A study of SDLC to develop well engineered software. Int. J. Adv. Res. Comput. Sci. **8**(3), 520–523 (2017)
23. Wagner, S.: Software Product Quality Control. Springer (2013)
24. Hu, R., et al.: Web Quality of Agile Web Development

Statistical Approach Based Cluster Head Selection in Heterogeneous Networks for IoT Applications

Seli Mohapatra(✉) and Prafulla Kumar Behera

Utkal University, Vanivihar, Bhubaneswar, Odisha, India

Abstract. Heterogeneous networks are energy constrained and requires clustering for load balancing with proper resource utilization. Moreover, development of different energy efficient technique has become a prime research topic now-a-days. Clustering algorithm in this context plays a vital role in selection and implementation of devices for tracking and monitoring of internet of things (IoT) applications. Selection of a proper cluster head (CH) helps in reducing energy consumption and increasing lifetime of the network. In this paper, statistical approach is followed for cluster head selection in R-LEACH protocol. Based on network state technique, the mean and variance of residual energy along with optimal parameter is considered that can make a smart system model with IoT products. The performance analysis of the proposed method is evaluated and compared to state-of-art LEACH and basic R-LEACH methods. An improvement in node utilization and energy utilization by 15% and 20% respectively is achieved.

Keywords: Heterogeneous network · Performance metrics · R-LEACH · Resource management · Statistical parameters

1 Introduction

Heterogeneous networks has become a potent and influential technology for utilizing platform and infrastructure as service for various IoT models that make the system smart. Different group of devices form an invisible and intelligent network capable of sensing, controlling, and communicating several applications, like monitoring and tracking. However, these services can be more efficient when proper resource management is provided. Again, the low power multifunctional devices creating IoT service requires a set of sensors to sense, collect, and forward relevant data to the base station. Base station processes and aggregates these data to backbone network for remote access. As per statistics, the IoT service has the ability to connect about 5 billion smart devices which will increases in future [1]. Hence, these devices need to be communicated virtually to the people that may create huge congestion in the network. Therefore, it becomes a requirement for developing heterogeneous network for basic node and energy utilization.

In comparison to homogeneous, the counterpart heterogeneous networks have a better communication impact due to its non-uniform energy and cost distribution among

© Springer Nature Singapore Pte Ltd. 2021
P. K. Behera and P. C. Sethi (Eds.): CSI 2020, CCIS 1372, pp. 27–35, 2021.
https://doi.org/10.1007/978-981-16-2723-1_4

the nodes. The complexity in design of hardware and selection of proper deployment strategy makes it more challenging [2]. Since the devices in the IoT service are of different variants, heterogeneous network design is more suitable for this purpose. Besides the main challenge owing to this network is the issue of scalability, energy distribution, security, lifetime maximization, data aggregation, and forwarding etc. Thus in order to achieve the required quality of service (QoS), node energy utilization is emphasized herein. It can be modified and modeled effectively by proper analysis of models based on control overhead, throughput, and packet reception rate. However, in realistic models the network bears more packet loss due to noise, interference, and other channel impairments. One of the basic approaches to deal with these problems is selection of an efficient protocol for transmission, reception, and propagation methods. The route selection and data forwarding criteria can be resolved by routing protocols. Moreover, hierarchical protocols exhibit low power transmission and reception. Clustering is one of the hierarchical techniques that involve different energy distribution for cluster head and cluster members. The basic LEACH (Low Energy Adaptive Clustering Hierarchy) defines the cluster head selection method efficiently. However, this method involves the cluster head selection on the distance criteria only that give low energy making it unsuitable for IoT devices. So, there is a requirement of modification in the routing strategy of LEACH which motivated us for improvisation in the protocol using the statistical analysis.

This paper focuses on the cluster head selection methods on the basis of energy distribution within the nodes. The contribution of this paper is to evaluate node state by considering statistical parameters along with residual energy and distance to sink. Furthermore, it tends to increase the data rate and network lifetime. The performance of the network is validated by observing the available alive nodes and dead nodes for several rounds under consideration for selecting cluster heads.

The rest of the paper is organized as Sect. 2 with basic background and related works. Our proposed model along with some existing model of LEACH is described in Sect. 3. Next, we analyzed and compared the proposed model with other state-of-art models and performance analysis as mentioned in Sect. 4 followed by conclusion in Sect. 5.

2   Related Works

The hierarchical protocols as a part of network structure based method for designing heterogeneous network is considered with implementation as described in several papers mentioned. The network is divided in form of different clusters on basis of arbitrary rules. In [3] authors described the location of cluster head within the cell of Voronoi structure with randomness. The nodes having the value less than special threshold level is set on the basis of lifetime and latency parameter.

Clustering algorithm provided energy efficient transmission of data from CH to base station with a uniform energy distribution among the nodes. One of the classical clustering approaches is LEACH [4], which helps in conserving network energy. The cluster head selection method in LEACH is based on uniform distribution of energy among the nodes. Cluster heads are selected with a probability P; if the total number of nodes in the network G is given by n and r is the current round; then the cluster head selection is based on the threshold parameter given by

$$T(n) = \begin{cases} \dfrac{P}{1-P\left(r \text{ mod } \left(\frac{1}{P}\right)\right)} & n \in G \\ 0, & otherwise \end{cases} \tag{1}$$

In this procedure, distances between the nodes are used as the basic rule. However, this does not satisfy the energy utilization of the network. EB-LEACH [5] is designed as well distributed cluster in the network that increases overall lifetime. The authors have emphasized on threshold based cluster head selection considering distance between node and base station. Thein et al, in [6] have implemented the residual energy as the basic probabilistic parameter to select CH. The authors have considered optimal cluster head selection criteria, but it was limited between 1 and 6. In another cluster head selection criteria is chosen where the threshold parameter is based on relative hotness of deployed node in the network.

Several optimization techniques like PSO and ACO are also incorporated in which the objective function decides the residual energy as well as node status for CH selection. However, these techniques are more time consuming with higher latency. A multi criteria based non-probabilistic cluster head selection method is also described in [7], where the network is associated with separate zones for cluster head discovery. Y. Jaradat et al [8] proposed a simulation model which evaluates the performance of a homogeneous LEACH protocol in a realistic noisy environment. With the variations of probabilistic distribution the energy model incorporating noise was derived analytically. Similarly, the current traffic situation is handled by advertising short beacon message containing information on speed, direction, position and other relevant safety information. Comparative analysis of various routing protocols is described on the basis of performance metrics in [9–11]. However in [12] the authors proposed multipath based multicast routing protocol analysis for energy efficiency purpose.

3 Proposed Model

In this section, we have proposed a hierarchical based LEACH model with statistical analysis based cluster head selection and compared for its analysis with other variants of LEACH protocol.

3.1 Overview

The proposed protocol model is based on the basic parameters that define the threshold value with more precise cluster head selection. Thus, the heterogeneous network so formed has improved energy efficiency and network lifetime. In this model, uneven energy distribution forms normal, advanced, and super sensor nodes. The advanced nodes have the capability of forming cluster head, whereas super node acts as a gateway or sink. Following assumptions are made for the development of the proposed model.

- Sensor nodes are static with an initial energy of 0.5 J. However the network is made heterogeneous with three different energy levels for normal, advanced and super nodes.

- Nodes deployment is random and data transmission is maintained periodically.
- Sink receives all data from cluster head and forwards it to the backbone network.

3.2 Radio Energy Model

The energy model used in a three level heterogeneous network is based on free space for short distance communication between nodes and cluster heads [2]. Multipath criteria for longer distance transmission between cluster head and sink in which distance d_0 is calculated from energy parameters associated with free space ε_{fs} and multipath parameter ε_{mp} respectively as follows

$$d_0 = \sqrt{\frac{\varepsilon_{fs}}{\varepsilon_{mp}}} \tag{2}$$

Now considering the transmitter and receiver electronics, for symmetrical propagation channel the power transmitting l bits of data in a packet to a sensor placed d meters away is represented as

$$E_{Tx}(l, d) = \begin{cases} l \times (E_{Tx} + E_{da}) + l \times \varepsilon_{mp} \times d^4, \, d > d_o \\ l \times (E_{Tx} + E_{da}) + l \times \varepsilon_{fs} \times d^2, \, d \leq d_o \end{cases} \tag{3}$$

$$E_{Rx}(l, d) = l \times (E_{Rx} + E_{da}) \tag{4}$$

In the above equation $E_{Tx}(l, d)$ and $E_{Rx}(l, d)$ refers to the energy transmitted and received respectively between two entities separated by d distance carrying l bits of information. On the basis of energy distribution nodes are randomly deployed in the network with one sink node at the highest energy followed by 20% of the total nodes whose energy is in between energy of normal nodes and sink node and the rest nodes are cluster members. The various steps followed in the implementation of the SR-LEACH approach are as follows

- *Step 1: Deployment Stage:* Nodes are deployed randomly with uneven energy distribution. Normal nodes assigned 0.5 J energy the lowest in network, whereas advanced and super nodes are assigned 30% and 50% more energy than normal nodes. Only CH has the capability to send data to base station at the center of network.
- *Step 2: Setup Stage:* First the clusters are formed using LEACH algorithm. The advanced nodes act as normal node if not selected as CH. In our work Sensor-Medium Access Control (SMAC) channel access strategy is used with sleep awake method for energy conservation.
- *Step 3: Cluster Head Selection Stage:* The CH is selected based on the residual energy of nodes in each round. Threshold values are updated regularly. When the residual energy becomes below the threshold value it becomes a normal node. It continues till all the nodes have a residual energy below threshold. The process of threshold value updating is carried out till all nodes are dead. The nodes are classified according to the mean, μ of residual energy E_{res} and variance σ^2 given as

$$\mu = \frac{1}{n} \sum_{i=1}^{n} E_{res}(i) \tag{5}$$

$$\sigma^2 = \frac{1}{m} \sum_{k=1}^{m} (E_{res}(k) - \mu(i)), \quad m \in n, n \in G \tag{6}$$

The low and high levels of the energy span are obtained from (5) and (6), and given as

$$E_{rlow}(i) = \mu(i) - \sigma(i) \tag{7}$$

$$E_{rhigh}(i) = \mu(i) + \sigma(i) \tag{8}$$

These energy spans change in each round depending on the number of alive nodes, residual energy variation, and number of death nodes. The mean and variance also changes in each round. Based on these energy spans the adaptive threshold value of SR-LEACH is given by

$$T_m(n) = \begin{cases} Pc \Big/ \big(1 - Pc(r \bmod 1/p_C)\big) \times \frac{E_{res}}{E_{amp}-E_o} \times k_{opt}, & m \in n, n \in G \\ 0; & Otherwise \end{cases} \tag{9}$$

Where $T(n)$ is the threshold parameter assigned considering m advanced nodes, E_{amp} is amplification energy and E_0 is the initial energy level. P_c is the probability of the advanced node considering the energy spans of the network presented as

$$P_c = P \times \frac{E_{rlow}}{E_{rhigh}} \tag{10}$$

The optimal number of clusters is represented as

$$k_{opt} = \sqrt{\frac{n}{2\pi}} \sqrt{\frac{\varepsilon_{fs}}{\varepsilon_{mp}} \frac{M}{d^{\alpha}}}, \quad \text{where} \quad \alpha = \begin{cases} 2, d \le d_o \\ 4, d > d_o \end{cases} \tag{11}$$

Where M represents network diameter and α is the RF attenuation co-efficient. Once CH is selected, it is advertises to members of the network. Depending on the signal strength the normal nodes decide to be included or excluded in that group. This process is repeated till all nodes exhaust their energies.

- Step 4: Steady State Stage: This stage is the data transmission state, where the cluster members sense the data and forward it to CH on the basis of Time Division Multiple Access (TDMA). When the first level data transfer is over, the CHs do the data processing by removal of relevant data in the cluster group. After data aggregation process CH forwards them to super node or gateway node for communication with backbone network.

The proposed energy efficient routing protocol is named as Statistical based Residual LEACH and referred as SR-LEACH throughout this paper.

4 Simulation and Result Analysis

In this section, the simulation and analysis of SR-LEACH is compared with other LEACH variants carried in MATLAB software is presented. The entire clustering model compared in our work has almost the same heterogeneous condition.

4.1 Simulation Environment and Performance Metrics

In the simulation 100 nodes are considers and deployed in a network area of 400×400 m^2. The link location is somehow fixed around center of the network field. The normal and advanced node is deployed randomly in a ratio of 5:1 with different energy distribution. In order to evaluate the performance, the network analysis is performed on the basis of residual energy, number of alive nodes, number of dead nodes, and number of packets sent with respect to the number of rounds. The other simulation parameters are represented in Table 1.

Table 1. Simulation parameters.

Parameters	Value
Packet Size	4000 bits
MAC Protocol	S-MAC
Routing protocol	LEACH, LEACH-EB, RLEACH, SR-LEACH
Channel	Phy wireless
Propagation model	Free Space
Deployment Model	Stationary
Initial Energy (Eo)	0.5 J
Transmitted Energy	50 pJ/bit/m^2
Received Energy	50 pJ/bit/m^2
Energy Dissipation: Free space	10 pJ/bit/m^2
Energy Dissipation: Multipath	0.0013 pJ/bit/m^4
Energy Dissipation: Power Amplifier	100 pJ/bit/m^2

4.2 Result Analysis

The simulation result of the heterogeneous network for $m = 0.4$ is discussed herein. The performance analysis of these protocols is categorized on the basis of network lifetime, energy efficiency, and data throughput of the network.

4.2.1 Network Lifetime

The lifetime of a network is analyzed on the basis of number of alive nodes and number of dead nodes in the network after certain iterations as shown in Fig. 1. The first node dies almost at the same state or round for LEACH EB, R- LEACH and SR-LEACH, but the rate of decay is less than that of standard LEACH. It is due to the fact that when energy model is considered for threshold selection it give better result than only distance criteria. However, considering the longevity of the network, the last node is dead at around 1032 whereas the last node dead is almost at around 2200 for LEACH EB and RLEACH. Comparing our model SR LEACH has still some nodes left even after 2500 rounds. Although there is a sharp decrease in alive nodes in the initial rounds due to the fact that control overhead is very high in residual based leach, but with increase in the number of rounds only a small factor of nodes participate in data forwarding operation that leads to the concept that the network failure is not caused easily. Again due to statistical approach, the node selection for data forwarding operation changes and it primarily focuses on energy efficient nodes. Hence the chance of network longevity is quite high in SR-LEACH compared to other variants. Similarly verifying our model with increase in dead node counts in Fig. 1, it is observed that even after 2500 rounds there is a chance of a very less number of nodes in the network, which indicates the heterogeneous network is not dead for considering SR LEACH.

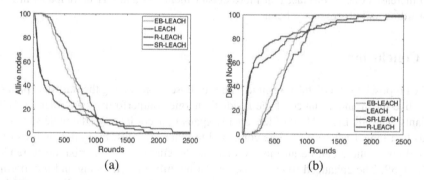

Fig. 1. Illustration of (a) Number of alive nodes, (b) Number of dead nodes vs Rounds

4.2.2 Energy Efficiency

The network energy efficiency is obtained from the average residual energy analysis of different variants of LEACH as depicted in Fig. 2. From the Fig. 2 (a) it is observed that when the number of rounds increases, there is a gradual decrease in the energy reserve parameter in each LEACH variant.

However, it is seen that the standard LEACH the network finishes much sooner than our proposed protocol. Almost after 1000 rounds the residual energy becomes constant, resulting in a longer network lifetime. The behavior of LEACH-EB and R-LEACH behaves almost equally in context to the residual energy parameter. From this result it is interpreted that our proposed model outperforms than other LEACH variants.

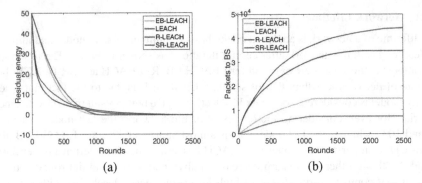

Fig. 2. Illustration of variation in (a) Residual Energy and (b) Packets sent to BS vs Rounds

4.2.3 Network Throughput

The network throughput is analyzed on the basis of number of effective packets sent to base station or sink node with respect to the variation of nodes as shown in Fig. 2. From the figure it is observed that since no energy parameter is considered so LEACH has very low throughput whereas SR-LEACH sends more number of packets to base station (BS) having more throughput. Moreover, with increase in number of rounds packet number also increases due to the fact that more cluster members and CH participates in data forwarding and processing scheme.

5 Conclusion

In the proposed protocol, the threshold value so chosen considering the statistical parameters like mean and variance of the residual energies outperforms than other LEACH variants. The SR-LEACH considers energy spans in accordance to the node state that leads to a longer network lifetime compared to other methods. From the analysis discussed above there can be an improvement in the energy span distribution to render better QoS. The enhanced routing process can be utilized in tracking and monitoring process for IoT applications. The model proposed can be tested on realistic scenarios also.

References

1. Gubbi, J., Buyya, R., Marusic, S., Palaniswami, M.: Internet of Things (IoT): a vision architectural elements, and future directions. Future Gener. Comput. Syst. **9**(7), 1645–1660 (2013)
2. Mohapatra, S., Mohapatra, R.K.: Comparative analysis of energy efficient MAC protocol in heterogeneous sensor network under dynamic scenario. In: 2017 2nd International Conference on Man and Machine Interfacing (MAMI), Bhubaneswar, pp. 1–5 (2017)
3. Kumar, V., Sandeep, D.N., Yadav, S., Barik, R.K., Tripathi, R., Tiwari, S.: Multi-hop communication based optimal clustering in hexagon and voronoi structured WSNs. AEU-Int. J. Electron. Commun. **93**, 305–316 (2018)

4. Singh, S.K., Kumar, P., Singh, J.P.: A Survey on successors of LEACH protocol. IEEE Access **5**, 4298–4328 (2017)
5. Feng, Y.F., Pan, S.G., Huang, Z.Y., Lin, H.C.: Improvement of energy efficiency in wireless sensor networks using low-energy adaptive clustering hierarchy (LEACH)-based energy betweeness model. Sens. Mater. **31**(9), 2691–2702 (2019)
6. Thein, M.C.M.,Thein, T.: An energy efficient cluster-head selection for wireless sensor networks. In: 2010 International Conference on Intelligent Systems, Modelling and Simulation (ISMS), Liverpool, UK, pp. 287–291 (2010)
7. Mansura, A., Drieberg, M., Abd Aziz, A., Bassoo, V.: Multi-energy threshold-based routing protocol for wireless sensor networks, pp. 71–75 (2019). https://doi.org/10.1109/ICSGRC.2019.8837090
8. Jaradat, Y., Masoud, M., Jannoud, I., Abu-Sharar, T., Zerek, A.: Performance analysis of homogeneous LEACH protocol in realistic noisy WSN. In: 2019 19th International Conference on Sciences and Techniques of Automatic Control and Computer Engineering (STA), Sousse, Tunisia, pp. 590–594 (2019)
9. Behera, T.M., Mohapatra, S.K., Samal, U.C., Khan, M.S., Daneshmand, M., Gandomi, A.H.: Residual Energy-based cluster-head selection in WSNs for IoT application. IEEE Internet Things J. **6**(3), 5132–5139 (2019)
10. Mohapatra, S., Kanungo, P.: Performance analysis of AODV, DSR, OLSR and DSDV routing protocols using NS2 Simulator. Procedia Eng. **30**, 69–76 (2012). ICCTSD 2012
11. Mohapatra, S., Kanungo, P.: Compartive performance analysis of MANET routing protocols using NS2 Simulator. In: Das, V.V., Thankachan, N. (eds.) Computational Intelligence and Information Technology. Communications in Computer and Information Science, vol. 250, pp. 731–736. Springer, Heidelberg (2011). https://doi.org/10.1007/978-3-642-25734-6_127
12. Mohapatra, S.: Performance analysis of multirate MM-OLSR protocol in wireless adhoc networks. In: 2017 International Conference on Wireless Communications, Signal Processing and Networking (WiSPNET), Chennai, pp. 1494–1499 (2017)

Remote Monitoring of Temperature Using Optical Fiber Bragg Grating Sensor

Sagupha Parween[(✉)] and Aruna Tripathy

College of Engineering and Technology, Bhubaneswar, Bhubaneswar, Odisha, India
atripathy@cet.edu.in

Abstract. Optical sensors are used to sense any change in environmental conditions. They utilize the measurand into changing some attributes of a light ray passing through an optical fiber. This change may be intensity, phase, state of polarization or a wavelength. This change is used for detection at the receiving end according to physical parameters. Fiber Bragg grating (FBG) sensors are one of the most commonly used sensors in optical communication. FBG sensor is mainly used for sensing temperature and strain. This paper focuses mainly on FBG optical sensor used as temperature sensor. The principle of FBG has been explained in detail for temperature sensing. The change in temperature with respect to change in thermo-optic coefficient has been analyzed. The sensed information has been retrieved at the user end using optical fiber cable (OFC) and free space optic (FSO) channels. A beam of light travelling through the OFC cable is called as a wired optical communication, whereas the FSO can be said as wireless communication. The performance of OFC and FSO channels has been compared for sensing the data from the FBG sensor using OptiSystem 16.0 Simulation Software. The contribution of the paper is threefold: (i) determination of the thermo optic coefficient and the range of temperature dependent on this coefficient for the FBG, (ii) comparison of the performances of sensed data transmission over OFC and FSO channel and (iii) evaluation of an analog link used to transmit and receive the measurand.

Keywords: Optical sensor · FBG · Thermo-optic coefficient · OFC · FSO

1 Introduction

An optical sensor has many advantages over electrical sensors such as high sensitivity, small size, no electromagnetic interference, resistance to corrosion, and its light weight [1]. Fibre Bragg Grating (FBG) sensors are mainly used for sensing temperature and strain with the additional advantages of low weight and small size as well as the capability of having multiple sensors in one line. The FBG sensor operates on the principle of Fresnel reflection wherein it uses the reflection and transmission of light when incident on an optical media having different refractive indices [1]. The FBGs or FBG arrays have been widely applied in the measurement of physical, chemical, biomedical, and electrical parameters where the information is usually encoded by the Bragg wavelength shift of

© Springer Nature Singapore Pte Ltd. 2021
P. K. Behera and P. C. Sethi (Eds.): CSI 2020, CCIS 1372, pp. 36–47, 2021.
https://doi.org/10.1007/978-981-16-2723-1_5

FBGs [2–5].The basic principle of FBG sensors is the measurement of an induced shift in the wavelength of an optical source due to a measurand, such as strain or temperature. A broadband light source i.e. optical spectrum given by a white light source is used to interrogate the grating, from which a narrowband slice is reflected and rest is transmitted [6]. White light source is a broadband light source which contains all the wavelengths [6]. When such a light is given as an input to the FBG sensor, any change in temperature with respect to the reference temperature will lead to reflect back the centre Bragg wavelength and pass the rest of the wavelengths. An FBG sensor thus, is said to work upon wavelength modulation. A basic block diagram of FBG sensor is given in Fig. 1.

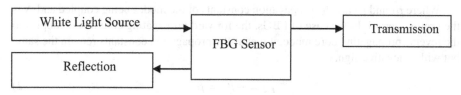

Fig. 1. Basic block diagram of FBG sensor

The sensed information is transmitted and subsequently received over an analog communication link which is realized by Optical Fiber Cable (OFC) and Free Space Optic (FSO) communication in this paper. The analog optical link has three sections: transmitter, optical fiber and receiver [7]. The transmitter basically provides electro-optic conversion; here we have used the sensed information of FBG sensor as an input to the OFC channel. The optical fiber takes the light beam to the destination. The receiver carries out the optoelectronic conversion by using photodiodes/photo detectors such as PIN photodiode and Avalanche photodiode [7, 8]. An FSO channel also has been used to transmit the sensed measurand to the receiver. The working of an FSO is similar to OFC with the only difference that the optical signal is sent through free air in the absence of optical cable [9, 10]. Section 2 describes about the FBG sensor system modeling. The results of experimental layouts for proposed FBG based system are shown in Sect. 3, the results and analysis of experimental arrangements are presented in Sect. 4. Section 5 provides a conclusion of the experimental results obtained.

2 System Model

An FBG is created by engraving periodic patterns of refractive index change inside the core of a single mode fiber. This change in refractive index is typically created by showing the fiber core to an intense interference pattern of UV energy [11]. The exposure produces a permanent increase in the refractive index of the fiber's core, creating a fixed index modulation according to the exposure pattern. This fixed index modulation is called a grating [12]. A small amount of light is reflected at each grating period. All the reflected light signals combine consistently to one large reflection at a particular wavelength. This is referred to as the Bragg condition, and the wavelength at which this reflection occurs is called the Bragg wavelength [12, 13].Only those wavelength are reflected that satisfy the Bragg condition and this wavelength has maximum efficiency [13].

When light from an optical white light source i.e. an optical spectrum is incident, only a specific wavelength which satisfies Bragg condition will be reflected while the remaining wavelengths are transmitted, the wavelength for which the incident light is reflected with maximum efficiency is called the Bragg wavelength. In optical fiber gratings, the phase matching condition is given by [14, 15].

$$\beta_1 - \beta_2 = \Delta\beta = \frac{2\pi}{\lambda} \tag{1}$$

Where β_1 and β_2 are the propagation constants of the modes being coupled and Λ is the grating period. In the case of FBGs, the forward propagating core mode couples to the reverse propagating core mode, it means the propagation constants remain the same but with a negative sign.

$$\beta_2 = -\beta_1 = \beta \tag{2}$$

Then the phase matching condition is given by,

$$\beta - (-\beta) = 2\beta = \frac{2\pi}{\Lambda} \tag{3}$$

But the propagation constant β is given by,

$$\beta = \frac{2\pi}{\lambda} n_{eff} \tag{4}$$

Where n_{eff} is the effective refractive index of fiber core, so Eq. (3) becomes

$$2\left(\frac{2\pi}{\lambda} n_{eff}\right) = \frac{2\pi}{\Lambda} \tag{5}$$

So the Bragg wavelength is given by [16, 17],

$$\lambda_B = 2n_{eff}\Lambda \tag{6}$$

From Eq. (6) we can see that Bragg wavelength will shift with respect to any change in effective refractive index or grating period. The effective refractive index has a value as average of all the periodic refractive indices in the optical fiber. The Bragg wavelength will shift with any change in the environmental conditions. As the Bragg wavelength depends upon effective refractive index n_{eff}, any change in effective refractive index will shift the Bragg wavelength. Any changes in the temperature of the surrounding from a reference level will lead to change in refractive index in the material; it means the effective refractive index will change. The change in effective refractive index is given by [19, 20],

$$n_{eff} = \xi n\Delta T \tag{7}$$

Where ξ is the thermo-optic coefficient, n is the refractive index of fiber, and ΔT is the change in temperature from the reference temperature. Equation (7) gives the change in temperature that will change the n_{eff} which leads to a shift in the Bragg wavelength.

3 Proposed System Using FBG

The layout of the proposed system to measure temperature using an FBG sensor system is shown in Fig. 2. Here the white light source (WLS) is given as an input to FBG sensor. In increasing or decreasing the temperature surrounding the grating from a reference temperature level, the refractive index of the fiber will experience a change as given in Eq. (7). Those wavelengths that satisfy the Bragg condition are reflected and rest is transmitted. The output spectrum of WLS, transmission and reflection can be seen through WDM FBG Sensor Interrogator as shown in Fig. 3(a), Fig. 3(b), and Fig. 3(c) respectively. If we increase or decrease the temperature the grating center wavelength will shift accordingly.

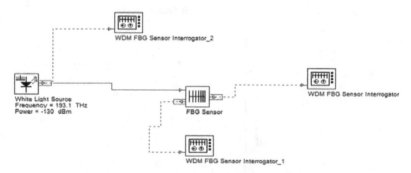

Fig. 2. Proposed system layout using an FBG sensor

We need to sense the temperature at the receiver through both the OFC and FSO link. The FBG output is transmitted over an analog link. In order to cover a large distance some suitable analog or digital modulation schemes may be employed. We have used amplitude modulation (AM) in our work here. The layouts of an OFC based link without and with AM are shown in Figs. 4 and 6 respectively. Similar schematic diagrams for an FSO based analog link are illustrated in Figs. 5 and 7 respectively.

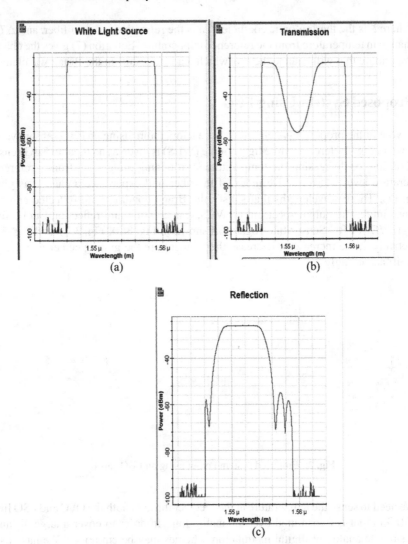

Fig. 3. (a) White light source signal spectrum; (b) Transmission signal spectrum; (c) Reflection signal spectrum

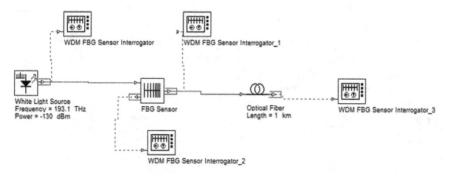

Fig. 4. Layout of FBG sensor system data sent through an OFC channel

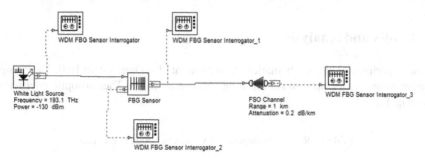

Fig. 5. Layout of FBG sensor system data sent through an FSO channel

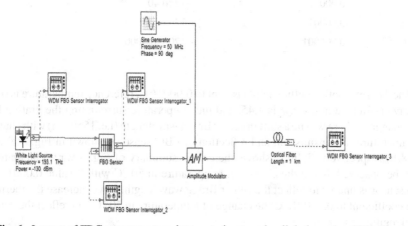

Fig. 6. Layout of FBG sensor system data sent via an analog link through a OFC channel

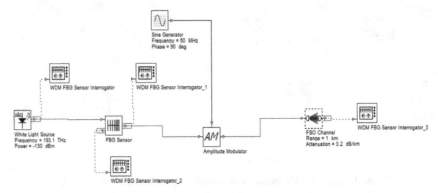

Fig. 7. Layout of FBG sensor system data sent via an analog link through a OFC channel

4 Results and Analysis

All the experimental block schematics are implemented in OptiSystem 16.0. The change in temperature varies up to a certain range according to the Thermo-optic coefficient shown in Table 1.

Table 1. Range of temperature vs. thermo-optic coefficient

Thermo-optic coefficient (/°C)	Range of temperature (°C)
0.0001	−12 to 40
0.00001	−120 to 400
0.000001	−1200 to 4000

The Thermo-optic coefficient (ξ) is kept to 0.0001/°C, reference temperature is 0°C, effective refractive index n_{eff} is 1.45, and the temperature surrounding the grating has been changed. There will be a shift in center Bragg wavelength (i.e. 1550 nm) with change in temperature in transmission and reflection of FBG sensor is shown in Fig. 8(a) and Fig. 8(b) respectively. Table 2 shows the colour summary of Fig. 8 w.r.t temperature. It can be observed that at the change of temperature in 50 °C with ξ value 0.0001, the FBG sensor is unable to reflect the center Bragg wavelength. If we increase the thermo-optic coefficient to 0.00001/°C the change of temperature in 50 °C can reflect the center wavelength.

The Bragg wavelengths will be shifted if we increase or decrease the temperature in the FBG sensor and send through OFC and FSO channel. The shift in Bragg wavelengths sensed by both OFC and FSO channel for layouts as shown in Figs. 4 and 5 for a length of 1 km with channel attenuation of value 0.2 dB/Km is compared and shown in Table 3. Table 4 shows the difference in Bragg wavelength shift with respect to center Bragg wavelength (i.e. 1.54999 μm) for reference temperature 0 °C, keeping ξ value 0.0001 and the temperature is changed according to the Table 3.

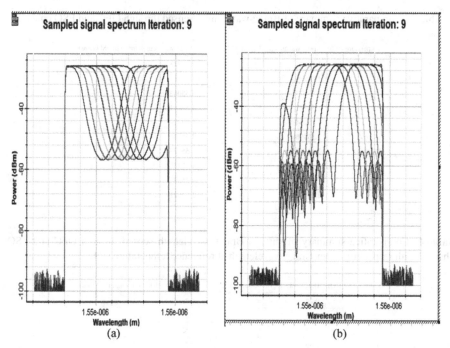

Fig. 8. (a) Transmission signal spectrum shift w.r.t change in temperature; (b) Reflection signal spectrum shift w.r.t change in temperature

Table 2. Colour summary of Fig. 8 w.r.t temperature

Colour	Temperature(°C)
	5
	10
	15
	20
	25
	30
	35
	40
	50

The change in wavelength w.r.t temperature is given by [21], the sample observation of theoretical and experimental wavelength shift is shown in Table 5.

$$(\Delta\lambda_B)_{temp} = \lambda_B(1 + \xi)\Delta T \qquad (8)$$

Figure 9 shows the comparative plot for temperature verses Bragg wavelength shift through OFC and FSO channels with respect to reference temperature 0 °C and $\lambda_B =$ 1.54999 μm (i.e. the center Bragg wavelength found experimentally).

Table 3. Comparative summary of Bragg wavelength sensed through OFC and FSO channel

Temperature (°C)	Bragg wavelength through OFC (μm)	Bragg wavelength through FSO (μm)
−5	1.54926	1.54923
0	1.54999	1.54999
5	1.55073	1.55069
10	1.55155	1.55154
15	1.55234	1.55229
20	1.55306	1.55311
25	1.55419	1.55427
30	1.55463	1.55465
35	1.55541	1.55535
40	1.55632	1.55621

Table 4. Comparative summary of shift in Bragg wavelength sensed through OFC and FSO channel with respect to center Bragg wavelength at reference temperature 0 °C

Temperature (°C)	Bragg wavelength through OFC (nm)	Bragg wavelength through FSO (nm)
−5	0.72	0.76
5	0.75	0.7
10	1.57	1.55
15	2.36	2.3
20	3.08	3.11
25	4.2	4.28
30	4.65	4.66
35	5.43	5.36
40	6.34	6.24

Table 5. Summary of theoretical and practical wavelength shift w.r.t temperature

Temperature (°C)	Theoretical ($\Delta\lambda_B$) (nm)	Experimental ($\Delta\lambda_B$) in OFC (nm)	Experimental ($\Delta\lambda_B$) in FSO (nm)
40	6.2	6.34	6.24
35	5.4	5.43	5.36
30	4.6	4.65	4.66

Figures 10(a) and 10(b) shows the attenuation verses distance to sense the transmitted data through OFC and FSO channel respectively.

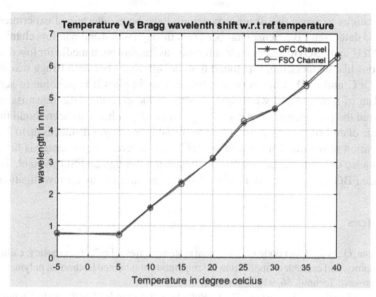

Fig. 9. Comparative plot of temperature vs. Bragg wavelength shift for OFC and FSO channel

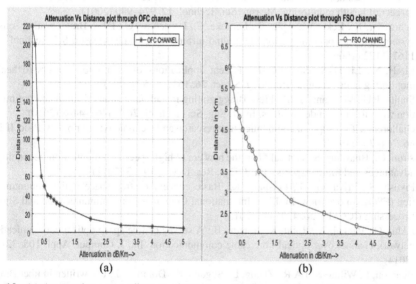

Fig. 10. (a) Attenuation verses distance plot to sense the transmitted data through OFC channel; (b) Attenuation verses distance plot to sense the transmitted data through FSO channel

5 Conclusion

The proposed layouts are implemented in OptiSystem 16.0 and the graphs are plotted using MATLAB R2016b. We have obtained the characteristics of FBG sensor by changing the temperature from −5 ℃ to 40 ℃. Thermo-optic coefficients for different range of temperatures to sense the Bragg wavelength have been determined experimentally. The sensed data from FBG Sensor has been sent through wired and wireless channel (i.e. through OFC and FSO) to assess their suitability as transmission media for low data rate applications like temperature. It is found that the difference between Bragg wavelength shifts in OFC and FSO is not very significant. This implies it is possible to send the sensed data of a measurand wirelessly in order to increase the data transmission rate and to avoid the presence of fiber cable. Experimentally, it has also been found that the sensed data of an FBG sensor can be retrieved reliably for longer distances up to 220 Km for attenuation of 0.1 dB/Km through an OFC cable whereas the coverage is limited to 6 Km distance only for the same value of attenuation through an FSO channel. The use of multiple FBG sensor based multiplexed system is currently under investigation.

References

1. Jonathan, O., et al.: Fiber optic measurement system for fresnel reflection sensing: calibration, uncertainty, and exemplary application in temperature-modulated isothermal polymer curing. J. Lightwave Technol. **36**, 939–945 (2018)
2. Ugis, S., Sandis, S., Vjaceslavs, B.: Evaluation and research of FBG optical temperature sensors network. In: Conference in Advances in Wireless and Optical Communications (2017)
3. Ecke, W., Latka, I., Willsch, R., Reutlinger, A., Graue, R.: Fibre optic sensor network for spacecraft health monitoring. Measur. Sci. Technol. **12**, 974–980 (2001)
4. Schroeder, K., Ecke, W., Apitz, J., Lembke, E., Lenschow, G.: Fibre Bragg grating sensor system monitors operational load in a wind turbine rotor blade. Measur. Sci. Technol. **17**, 1167–1172 (2006)
5. Li, H.-N., Li, D.-S., Song, G.-B.: Recent applications of fiber optic sensors to health monitoring in civil engineering. Eng. Struct. **26**, 1647–1657 (2004)
6. Sunita, P.U., Vivekanand, M.: Fiber Bragg grating modeling, characterization and optimization with different, index profiles. Int. J. Eng. Sci. Technol. **2**(9), 4463–4468 (2010)
7. Giallorenzi, T.G.: Optical communications research and technology: fiber optics. Proc. IEEE **66**, 744–780 (1978)
8. Arun, G., Bhawana, S.: Optical fiber: the new era of high speed communication (technology, advantages and future aspects). Int. J. Eng. Res. Dev. **4**, 19–23 (2012)
9. Piyush, S., Priyanka, G., Prashant, R.: Basic concept of free space optics communication (FSO): an overview. In: IEEE International Conference on Communication and Signal Processing (ICCSP), pp. 439–442 (2015)
10. Akhil, G., Pankaj, A., Rohit, K., Sonam, B.: A survey of free space optical communication network channel over optical fibre cable communication. Int. J. Comput. Appl. **105**, 32–36 (2014)
11. Bennion, I., Williams, J.A.R., Zhang, L., Sugden, K., Doran, N.J.: UV written in fiber Bragg gratings. Opt. Quantum Electron. **28**, 93–135 (1996). https://doi.org/10.1007/BF00278281
12. Hill, K.O., Meltz, G.: Fiber Bragg grating technology fundamentals and overview. J. Lightwave Technol. **15**, 1263–1276 (1997)
13. Sunita, P.U., Vivekanand, M.: Optimization of apodized fiber Bragg grating for sensing applications. Int. J. Comput. Appl. Electron. Inf. Commun. Eng. (ICEICE) **3** (2011)
14. Raman, K., Jose, M.L.H.: Handbook of Optical Fiber Sensing Technology; Fiber Grating Technology: Theory, Photosensitivity, Fabrication and Characterization, pp. 349–377. Wiley (2002)
15. Raman, K.: Fiber Bragg Gratings, 2nd edn. Academic Press, Cambridge (2010)

16. Carlo, E.C., Antonello, C., Clarissa, C., Abdulkadir, Y., Vittorio, M.N.P.: Fibre Bragg Grating Based Strain Sensors: Review of Technology and Applications. Sensors **18**, 1–27 (2018)
17. Cong, J., Zhang, X., Chen, K., Xu, J.: Fiber optic Bragg grating sensor based on hydrogels for measuring salinity. Sens. Actuators B Chem. **87**(9), 487–490 (2002)
18. Turan, E.: Fiber grating spectra. J. Lightwave Technol. **15**, 1277–1294 (1997)
19. Manish, S., Anubhuti, K.: Fiber Bragg Grating (FBG) is used as modeling and simulation for temperature sensor. Orient. J. Comput. Sci. Technol. **3**(1), 103–107 (2010)
20. Lun, K.C., Remco, N., Kevin, A.: Fiber Bragg grating sensors. In: Proceedings of the Symposium on IEEE Photonics Benelux, Netherlands (2010)
21. Khare, R.P.: Fiber Optics and Optoelectronics. Oxford University Press, Oxford (2004)

G-NSVF: A Greedy Algorithm for Non-Slicing VLSI Floorplanning

B. N. B. Ray, Sony Snigdha Sahoo$^{(\boxtimes)}$, and Susil Kumar Mohanty

Department of Computer Science and Applications, Utkal University,
Vani Vihar, Bhubaneswar 751004, Odisha, India

Abstract. Floorplanning is the first step in the physical design of VLSI. At this stage, the circuit is partitioned into blocks for packing them optimally within the chip. The metrics minimized in floorplan are overall interconnect wirelength, area of the chip, deadspace, etc. B* tree is a popular representation of floorplan as it captures both slicing and non-slicing floorplans. In this work, we have proposed a greedy algorithm for the initial floorplan, which can be used by simulated annealing placer that takes B* tree as the initial floorplan. The proposed algorithm in conjunction with B* tree when integrated into simulated annealing placer and experimented on MCNC benchmarks reduces the overall wirelength on an average by 11% and 69% as compared to random and prior greedy initial floorplans.

Keywords: B* Tree · Floorplanning · Greedy algorithm · Physical design

1 Introduction

Advancement in technology is leading to complex circuit design. VLSI floorplanning is an effective approach toward managing circuit design complexity. Given a set of circuit components or modules and a netlist specifying the interconnections between the modules, floorplanning ensures that none of the modules overlap each other and various metrics like area, total interconnect wirelength among modules are minimized.

Effective representation of such floorplans is important for ensuring the conversion between a representation and the corresponding floorplan. There are two basic floorplanning structures, namely slicing and non slicing floorplans. A brief comparison among the two has been given in [3]. Several representations have been proposed for representing non-slicing floorplans such as sequence pair [4], bounded slice line grid [5], O-tree [6], B*tree [1] etc. B* tree representation, as proposed by Chang et al. [1] has been proven to be an efficient representation of floorplan as it has many advantages over other representations. It has not only inherited all the best features of an ordered binary tree but also, is quite flexible in handling floorplanning problem with different kind of modules like hard, soft, preplaced, and rectilinear. It is very fast and can be easily implemented. The

© Springer Nature Singapore Pte Ltd. 2021
P. K. Behera and P. C. Sethi (Eds.): CSI 2020, CCIS 1372, pp. 48–58, 2021.
https://doi.org/10.1007/978-981-16-2723-1_6

authors in [9] have introduced following greedy evaluation function V_i for each module v_i for $(1 \leq i \leq n)$, n being the number of modules.

$$V_i = \lambda_1 \times \frac{h_i \times w_i}{H \times W} + \lambda_2 \times \frac{h_i + w_i}{H + W} \tag{1}$$

Where h_i and w_i are height and width of module v_i and H and W are the height and width of the floorplanning region. The constants $0 \leq \lambda_1, \lambda_2 \leq 1$ are such that $\lambda_1 + \lambda_2 = 1$. On the basis of the decreasing values of V_i for each $1 \leq i \leq n$ as given by Eq. 1, they generated an initial floorplan and represented the floorplan as B* tree. Their experimental results on MCNC Benchmarks using HSA (Hybrid Simulated Annealing) algorithm show improvement in overall interconnection wirelength and deadspace.

In this paper, we have introduced a greedy heuristic for initial floorplan modifying Eq. 1, so that it can be used by simulated annealing placer that takes the initial floorplan as a B* tree. The experimental results for our initial greedy floorplan on MCNC benchmarks [13] using B* tree based simulated annealing placer [1] reduce the final wirelength of floorplan on average by 11% and 69% respectively compared to floorplans generated randomly and also by Eq. 1, respectively.

In short, our contributions in this paper are listed below:

- We have proposed a greedy heuristic for the initial floorplan as an input to the simulated annealing placer.
- We have also integrated it into annealing based placer that takes initial floorplan as B* tree.
- Experimental results on MCNC benchmarks for the proposed initial greedy floorplan on an average show 11% and 69% reduction in placement wirelength compared to the random floorplan and also floorplan due to Eq. 1 respectively. In addition to this, the new heuristics also reduces the dead-space of final placement almost 3× than that of existing schemes.

The remaining of the paper is organized as follows. Section 2 gives a brief review of B* tree representation and simulated annealing algorithm for solving the floorplan problem. Section 3 begins with the problem statement, followed by our greedy approach. The implementation details are given in Sect. 4. The paper concludes with its future scope in Sect. 5.

2   B* Tree Representation

B* tree can be constructed along the same lines as that of the DFS procedure [1]. As proposed in [1] "first, the left subtree is recursively constructed starting from the root and then the right subtree. Let R_i be the set of modules located on the right-hand side and adjacent to a module b_i denoting the node n_i. The left child of the node n_i corresponds to the lowest module in R_i that has not been visited. The right child of n_i represents the module located above and adjacent to b_i, with its x-coordinate equal to that of b_i and its y-coordinate less than that of the top boundary of the module on the left-hand side and adjacent to b_i, if any [1]. The B*-tree maintains the geometric relationship between two modules as follows. If node n_j is the left child of node n_i, module b_j must be located on the right-hand side and adjacent to module b_i in the admissible placement; i.e., $x_j = x_i + w_i$. Besides, if node n_j is the right child of n_i, module b_j must be located above and adjacent to module b_i, with the x-coordinate of b_j equal to that of b_i; i.e., $x_j = x_i$. Also, since the root of T represents the bottom-left module, the x- and y-coordinates of the module associated with the root$(x\_root, y\_root) = (0,0)$". Primitive operations like insertion, the search can be performed in constant time, and deletion can be done in linear time on a B*tree. Apart from these, three new operations have been proposed for perturbing a B* tree in [8], namely rotation of a block, movement of a block from one place to another, and swapping of two blocks. These operations can be carried out in O(h) time, where h denotes the height of the B*tree.

2.1   Simulated Annealing Based B* Tree Representation

VLSI floorplanning being an NP-hard problem, various heuristic methods have been suggested for dealing with it. They can be categorized as constructive methods and iterative methods. The constructive methods use heuristic information for constructing the floorplan, whereas, the iterative ones make use of metaheuristic strategies, such as genetic algorithm, simulated annealing, and tabu search for obtaining good solutions. Floorplan algorithms used in [10] and [11] are also based on the simulated annealing. Simulated annealing (SA) is one of the widely used techniques used for approximating global optimization in a large search space [9]. However classical SA process has a significant draw-back of excessive running time. Thus, several annealing schemes for controlling the temperature changes during the annealing process have been proposed to reduce the running time of SA while searching for desired solutions more efficiently. One of the most successful among them has probably been the annealing schedule used by TimberWolf [7]. It provides not only the relative positions of the modules, but also their aspect ratios and pin positions. In [12], a fast simulated annealing algorithm has been proposed, which is significantly different from the existing simulated annealing schemes. It tries to speed up the annealing process. Hybrid simulated annealing approach in [9] constructs the initial B* tree using a new greedy approach, and a new operation on B* tree has also been proposed for exploring the search space. It leads to a much quicker optimal solution.

2.2   Original Algorithm

According to [9] "given an initial floorplan encoded in B* trees, at each temperature, the local search method finds a locally optimal solution through systematically examining those B* trees obtained by rotating a module by 90°, moving a module to another place or swapping two modules". If one of the operations leads to a floorplan with a smaller cost, the floorplan is accepted. The pseudo-code of the local search algorithm is presented in Algorithm 1 [9].

Algorithm 1: Algorithm for Local Search

1: I is an initial configuration
2: T is the Temperature
3: $mt = 0$, $uphill = 0$, $reject = 0$
4: $N^{max} = k \times m$
5: An empty list $LIST$
6: **while** $((uphill^{max})$ and $(mt < 2 \times N^{max}))$ **do**
7:     Randomly use one of the three operations to generate a new configuration J
8:     Calculate $cost(J)$, and update the cost to the list $LIST$
9:     $mt = mt + 1$
10:     $\Delta C = cost(J) - cost(I)$
11:     **if** $(\Delta C \leq 0)$ **then**
12:         $I = J$
13:         $localbest = J$
14:     **else**
15:         Randomly generate a number t $(0 \leq t \leq 1)$
16:         **if** $(t < e^{\frac{\Delta C}{T}})$ **then**
17:             $I = J$
18:             $uphill = uphill + 1$
19:         **else**
20:             $reject = reject + 1$
21:         **end if**
22:     **end if**
23: **end while**
24: $reject\_rate = \frac{reject}{mt}$
25: **return** configuration I, $reject\_rate$, $localbest$

After the local search, simulated annealing is used as a global search method to explore the search space [9].

Algorithm 2: Simulated Annealing Algorithm

1: Initial B^* tree B (By Algorithm 1)
2: $best = B$, $count = 0$
3: $conv\_rate = 1$, min
4: An initial temperature T
5: **while** $((reject\_rate < conv\_rate)$ and $(actual\_T > term\_T))$ **do**
6:     $count = count + 1$
7:     Optimize I using the Algorithm 1
8:     **if** $(cost(localbest) < cost(best))$ **then**
9:         $best = localbest$
10:     **end if**
11:     Update T and $actual\_T$
12:     **if** $(count > min)$ **then**
13:         $conv\_rate = 0.95$
14:     **end if**
15: **end while**

---

3 Problem Formulation

Let $M = \{v_1, v_2, \cdots, v_n\}$ be a set of modules with height h_i and width w_i and N be the Net-list for specifying interconnection among the modules. A floorplan F assigns M onto a plane in such a manner that none of the modules overlap each other. Area A of a floorplan F is a measure of the area of the smallest rectangle that surrounds all the modules. Wirelength W is the interconnection cost, and it is a measure of the total wirelength for maintaining the connection specified by N. The cost of a floorplan as given in [9] is given by the following equation.

$$f = w \times \frac{area(F)}{norm\_area} + (1-w) \times \frac{wirelength(F)}{norm\_wirelength}$$

where w and (1-w) are weights such that $w \in [0, 1]$ assigned for minimizing area and interconnection. This cost function has been adopted in [9]. A floorplan is said to be compact if no modules can be moved left or down without moving other modules. A compact floorplan can be represented using B* tree. The solution space is composed of all the B* trees that can be constructed when modules are given. As there exists a unique B* tree for every compacted floorplan, redundant solutions in the search space are eliminated.

3.1   Our Proposed Greedy Algorithm

This section proposes a modified heuristic cost function for the initial floorplan representation of the B* tree.

For generating the initial floorplan, the heuristic cost function defined by Eq. 1 has been modified as below. For each module v_i, the evaluation function say f_{v_i} is defined as

$$f_{v_i} = \lambda_1 \times \frac{h_i \times w_i}{H \times W} + \lambda_2 \times \frac{h_i + w_i}{H + W} + \frac{no\_of\_pins_i}{total\_no\_of\_pins} \tag{2}$$

where $0 \leq \lambda_1, \lambda_2 \leq 1$ are non negative weights such that $\lambda_1 + \lambda_2 = 1$. and have been set to 0.5 each as has been adopted in [9]. And $no\_of\_pins_i$ is the number pins of each module v_i, while $total\_no\_of\_pins$ is the summation of pins of each of the modules.

This cost function is calculated for every module. Modules are then packed in decreasing order of their heuristic values.

The heuristic function given by Eq. 1 normalizes area as VLSI floorplanning has always focused on minimization of area and wirelength. But the proposed approach has considered area, wirelength and pin density of each module together. A module with larger f_{v_i} is packed earlier i.e. modules are packed in decreasing order of f_{v_i} values.

3.2   Greedy Algorithm

The following Greedy_initial_placer() algorithm places modules according to decreasing value of f_{v_i}.

Algorithm 3: Greedy_initial_placer()

1: **for** i = 1 to n **do**
2:    Module v_i, calculate $f_{v_i} = \lambda_1 \times \frac{h_i \times w_i}{H \times W} + \lambda_2 \times \frac{h_i + w_i}{H+W} + \frac{no\_of\_pins_i}{total\_no\_of\_pins}$
3: **end for**
4: Sort f_{v_i} in decreasing order $\forall_{i=1}^{n} v_i$
5: Let $M' = \{v_1', v_2', \cdots, v_n'\}$ be the permutation of $M = \{v_1, v_2, \cdots, v_n\}$ resulting from step 4
6: Call $Place\_Module(M')$ to place modules in layout area

The procedure $Place\_Module(M')$ places modules in the prescribed order of M' within the chip and returns the initial B* tree B for the simulated annealing placer. While placing modules in the chip, the procedure $Place\_Module(M')$ uses the following operations, as discussed in [9]. If B is the set of modules placed in the chip, then the feasible region of the chip is the free space in the chip where if a module is placed, then it neither overlaps with any modules of B nor it oversteps the floorplan area.

1. Determine points in the feasible region and sort them in their increasing order of y-coordinates and then choose the point in that order.
2. Then choose the module from M' and put at the bottom left corner of that feasible point and include the module in set B. Then delete placed module from the set M'.
3. If at that feasible point determined in step 1, no module can be placed, then exclude that feasible point and select the next feasible point in the sorted order and then goto step 2.
4. Continue to step 2 and step 3 until M' is empty.

At the end of step 4, the initial greedy B* for the annealing placer is returned. The pseudo-code $Place\_Module(M')$ is described by Algorithm 4.

Algorithm 4: Place_Module(M')

1: $M' = \{v'_1, v'_2, \cdots, v'_n\}$
2: Initialize B* tree $B = Nil$
3: **while** $(M' \neq \phi)$ **do**
4:     Execute steps 1), 2), 3) for selecting a feasible point p_i and a module v'_i;
5:     Put v'_i at point p_i, then remove v'_i from M' and add it to B
6: **end while**
7: **return** B* tree B

3.3 Time Complexity Analysis

In Algorithm 3, the step 4 involves $O(nlogn)$ comparisons for sorting f_{v_i} ($1 \leq i \leq n$), the heuristic values f_{v_i}. The procedure $Place\_Module(M')$ (Algorithm 4) at step 6 uses $O(nlogn)$ comparisons for sorting y-coordinates of n feasible points and $O(n)$ time to place n modules in B* tree B. Thus the running time of Greedy_initial_placer() Algorithm $= O(nlogn) + O(nlogn) + O(n) = O(nlogn)$.

After the modules are packed according to the above Algorithm 3 (see Fig. 1), it is then converted into B* tree, as shown in Fig. 2. Then Algorithm 1 and Algorithm 2 are used to find the solution of the floorplan.

Before we discuss the effect of various initial floorplans on the quality of the final floorplan, we use the following additional notations.

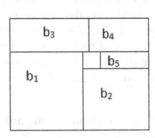

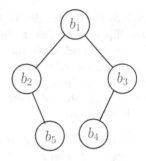

Fig. 1. Floorplan   **Fig. 2.** B* Tree of the Floorplan

- B*tree WL(B* tree Deadspace): final floorplan wirelength (Dead space) due to random initial floorplan given as an input to B* tree-based simulated annealing placer [1]
- HSA WL(HSA Deadspace): final floorplan wirelength (Deadspace) due to initial floorplan of Eq. 1
- Proposed WL(Proposed Deadspace): final floorplan wirelength (Deadspace) due to initial floorplan of Eq. 2.

4   Performance of the Proposed Greedy Approach

In order to study the efficacy of the proposed greedy strategy against random initial floorplan and floorplan due to Eq. 1, we implemented the proposed greedy algorithm and the greedy algorithm of Eq. 1 in C++. We integrated them into the publicly available B* tree-based simulated annealing placer [1]. For simulation purposes, we have used the MCNC floorplan benchmark suite [13]. All experiments were conducted on a Linux machine with a Core i5 processor, with a speed of 2.3 GHz and 4GB RAM. We have conducted three sets of experiments on MCNC benchmarks. In our first set of experiments, we presented the random floorplan of benchmark circuits as input to the B* tree-based simulated annealing placer as used in [1]. For the second set of experiments, we repeated the first experiment providing benchmark circuits as input to the annealing placer based on a greedy strategy of Eq. 1. And for the third set of experiments, we provided benchmark circuits as input to the placer based on our greedy strategy given by Eq. 2. The experimental results for wirelength and deadspace for various circuits for these three sets of experiments are presented in Table 1 and Table 2, respectively.

In Table 1, the names of circuits are put in the first row, starting from column 2 through column 6. The second row of the table presents final wirelengths (B* tree WL) of floorplans in millimeter for various circuits from column 2 through column 6 based on random floorplan. The second row presents final floorplans wirelengths (HSA WL) for the greedy algorithm on the framework of Eq. 1. And the third row shows the final placement wirelength on the basis of our

Table 1. B* Tree, HSA and proposed algo wirelength result

Circuit	ami33	ami49	apte	hp	xerox	Norm_WL
B*tree WL	178.139	11460.6	1058.36	317.894	1162.141	1.116
HSA WL	170.317	8818.91	1112.05	1136.8	1098.19	1.69
Proposed WL	170.317	8818.91	1018.5	267.51	1151.44	1

Table 2. B* Tree, HSA, proposed algo deadspace result

Circuit	ami33	ami49	apte	hp	xerox	Norm_DS
B*Tree Deadspace	5.56	46.89	2.03	23.87	6.21	2.93
HSA Deadspace	6.06	29.95	2.03	24.69	4.19	2.92
Proposed Deadspace	6.06	29.95	3.44	2.23	7.04	1

Table 3. Computation statistics for random initial floorplan

Circuit	ami33	ami49	apte	hp	xerox
No of modules	33	49	9	11	10
Height	1.715	39.074	14.918	3.766	7.966
Width	0.714	1.708	3.186	3.08	2.59
Area	1.22451	66.738	47.53	11.599	20.632
Wirelength	178.139	11460.6	1058.36	317.894	1162.141
Total Area	1.156	35.445	46.562	8.83	19.350
Deadspace	5.56	46.89	2.03	23.87	6.21
CPU Time	2.39	30.74	1.94	1.34	0.27
Last CPU Time	2.37	27.89	0.18	1.12	0.23

Table 4. Computation statistics for initial floorplan based on Greedy HSA

Circuit	ami33	ami49	apte	hp	xerox
No of modules	33	49	9	11	10
Height	0.679	29.624	3.186	21.476	2.59
Width	1.813	1.708	14.918	0.546	7.798
Area	1.23103	50.5978	47.5287	11.7259	20.197
Wirelength	170.317	8818.91	1112.05	1136.8	1098.19
Total Area	1.156	35.445	46.562	8.83	19.350
Deadspace	6.06	29.95	1.89	24.69	4.19
CPU Time	2.77	29.07	0.14	4.22	0.29
Last CPU Time	2.74	24.05	0.21	0.37	0.29

Table 5. Computation statistics for proposed Greedy initial floorplan

Circuit	ami33	ami49	apte	hp	xerox
No of modules	33	49	9	11	10
Height	0.679	29.624	13.182	2.016	2.604
Width	1.813	1.708	3.658	4.48	7.994
Area	1.23103	50.5978	48.2198	9.032	20.816
Wirelength	170.317	8818.91	1018.5	267.51	1151.44
Total Area	1.156	35.445	46.562	8.83	19.350
Deadspace	6.06	29.95	3.44	2.23	7.04
Last CPU Time	2.74	24.05	0.09	0.14	0.20

greedy algorithm given by Eq. 2. From Table 1, it is clear that for all circuits, the proposed greedy initial floorplan consistently reduces the final placement wirelength. Column 7 of Table 1 displays the normalized wirelengths (Nor_WL) of B* tree WL, HSA WL, and Proposed WL. From column 7, one can see that the proposed greedy approach, on an average reduces the final placement wirelength by 11% and 69%, respectively, as compared to the random floorplan and greedy floorplan due to Eq. 1. This is also evident from the bar graph shown in Fig. 3, where the x-axis represents benchmarks and y-axis wirelength. In Fig. 3, blue bar, red bar and gray bar correspond to B*tree WL, HSA WL, and Proposed WL, respectively.

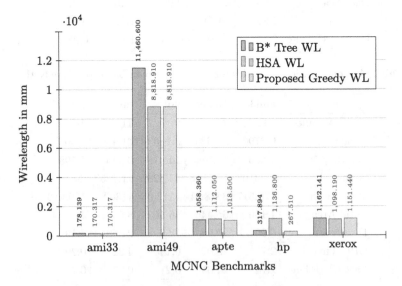

Fig. 3. Plot representing B* Tree wirelength, Greedy HSA wirelength and that obtained in the Proposed Greedy Approach (Color figure online)

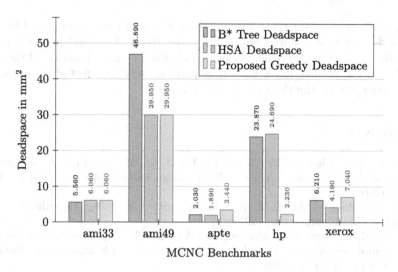

Fig. 4. Plot representing B* Tree deadspace, Greedy HSA deadspace and that obtained in the Proposed Greedy Approach (Color figure online)

Table 2 presents the results for deadspace of final floorplans for various circuits by initial floorplans generated randomly by Eq. 1 and by Eq. 2 (proposed greedy algorithm). Here also column 7 presents normalized deadspace of final floorplans by three approaches. From Table 2, it is evident that the deadspace of final floorplans due to the random floorplan and HSA based floorplan are almost $3\times$ more than that of the proposed greedy floorplan. This fact is also illustrated by bar graph shown in Fig. 4, where the x-axis represents benchmarks and y-axis deadspace. In Fig. 4, blue bar, red bar and gray bar correspond to B*tree Deadspace, HSA Deadspace, and Proposed Deadspace, respectively. Table 3, Table 4, and Table 5 show computation statistics (such as Height, Width, Area, Wirlength, Deadspace, and CPU time of final floorplan) for random, greedy HSA and proposed greedy initial floorplans. The consistent decrease in wirelength and deadspace of the final floorplan for the proposed greedy initial floorplan may be attributed to the fact that the proposed strategy is more amenable to generate initial floorplan that is close to the optimal, which is the biggest advantage of the algorithm. It is interesting to explore the nature of the cost function surface on the basis of various greedy approaches to the initial floorplan.

5   Conclusion and Future Scope

In this work, we have proposed a greedy heuristic for the initial floorplan, which can be used as an input by any simulated annealing placer. The proposed greedy floorplan, when given as an input to simulated annealing placer based on B* tree representation, shows a good reduction in wirelength as well as dead space compared to the random floorplan and prior art on the greedy floorplan. Experimental results on MCNC benchmarks for the proposed greedy approach on an average reduces final floorplan wirelength by 11% and 69% as compared to random and prior greedy initial floorplans, respectively. The deadspace produced by random and prior greedy floorplans are almost 3× more than that of the proposed greedy approach. In the future, we plan to study the effect of the proposed greedy floorplan on the thermal aware floorplan.

References

1. Chang, Y.C., Chang, Y.W., Wu, G.M., Wu, S.W.: B* Tree: a new representation for non slicing floorplans. In: ACM/IEEE Design Automation Conference, pp. 458–463 (2000)
2. Chen, J., Zhu, W., Ali, M.M.: A Hybrid Simulated Annealing Algorithm for Non-slicing VLSI Floorplanning (2011)
3. Chan, H.H., Adya, S.N., Markov, I.L.: Are floorplan representations important in digital design?. In: Proceedings of the International Symposium on Physical Design, pp. 168–173 (2000)
4. Murata, H., Fujiyoshi, K., Nakatake, S., Kajitani, Y.: Rectangle-packing based module placement. In: Proceedings of the ICCAD, pp. 472–479 (1995)
5. Nakatake, S., Fujiyoshi, K., Murata, H., Kajitani, Y.: Module placement on BSG-structure and IC layout applications. In: Proceedings of the ICCAD, pp. 484–491 (1996)
6. Guo, P.-N., Cheng, C.-K., Yoshimura, T.: An O-tree representation of non-slicing floorplan and its applications. In: Proceedings of the DAC, pp. 268–273 (1999)
7. Sechen, C., Sangiovani-Vincentelli, A.L.: The timber wolf placement and routing package. IEEE J. Solid-State Circuits SC-20(2), 510–522 (1985)
8. Chen, J., Liu, Y., Zhu, Z., Zhu, W.: An adaptive hybrid memetic algorithm for thermal-aware non-slicing VLSI floorplanning. Integr. VLSI J. 58 (2017). https://doi.org/10.1016/j.vlsi.2017.03.006
9. Chen, J.Z., Ali, W., Montaz, A.: A hybrid simulated annealing algorithm for non slicing VLSI floorplanning. IEEE Trans. Syst. Man Cybern Part C: Appl. Rev. 41, 544–553 (2011). https://doi.org/10.1109/TSMCC.2010.2066560
10. Sur-Kolay, S.: Studies on nonslicible floorplans in VLSI layout design. Ph.D. dissertation, Department of Computer Science and Engineering, Jadavpur University, Calcutta (1991)
11. Wong, D.F., Liu, C.L.: Floorplan design for rectangular and L-shaped modules. In: Proceedings of the International Conference on Computer Aided Design, pp. 520–523, November 1987
12. Chen, T.C., Chang, Y.-W.: Modern floorplanning based on fast simulated annealing, pp. 104–112 (2005). https://doi.org/10.1145/1055137.1055161
13. The MCNC Benchmark Problems for VLSI Floorplanning. http://www.mcnc.org

Cloud Service Selection Using Fuzzy ANP

Konatham Sumalatha[1]($\boxtimes$) (iD) and M. S. Anbarasi[2]

[1] Department of Computer Science and Engineering, Pondicherry Engineering College,
Pondicherry, India
[2] Department of Information Technology, Pondicherry Engineering College, Pondicherry, India
anbarasims@pec.edu

Abstract. In current scenario cloud computing has become emerging technology, as it provides services on computing (C) and non-computing (NC) resources to the government, private organization and also individuals based on pay-for-utility policy. Hardware and software resources are delivered as virtualized services. But selecting a best cloud provider is a challenging and complex task for consumers as it includes more providers with diverse configurations. Since it involves multiple criteria towards consumer perception of QoS, in-depth research is required. To provide solution for multi criteria decision making in nature, we propose ANP (Analytic Network Process) method integrated with fuzzy perception. The experimental studies shows the improved results and validity of proposed method.

Keywords: Cloud computing · Fuzzy inference · ANP · Customer feedback · Multi Criteria Decision Making

1 Introduction

A utility computing [1] called cloud computing provides a huge collection of services to customers on pay-as-you-go [2] phenomena. Many organizations are migrating their IT applications from static environment to dynamic environment where provisioning resources using virtualization. It provisions virtualized resources like CPU, storage, network, databases, application server, and internet server, etc. Cloud service providers like Rackspace, Google, IBM, Amazon etc. are offering pool of different services based on demand. Basically, customers have different requirements to develop their applications. Different configurations of VMs from Azure required (based on workload) for different applications as shown in Table 1.

Choosing the right mix of services is a challenging task for the customers as it includes heterogeneity [3]. Due to heterogeneity of configurations, selecting QoS optimized cloud service isn't an easy task [4]. A high end Amazon EC2 CPU response is 20% less expensive than the comparable low-end Microsoft Azure. But its speed of processing application's workload is very high. This configuration information is available in provider's website for reference. Due to combination of inconsistent criteria, the information provided by website is not sufficient for comparison. And also the provider's published data is not trustworthy as they overemphasize their services. However, this

P. K. Behera and P. C. Sethi (Eds.): CSI 2020, CCIS 1372, pp. 59–70, 2021.
https://doi.org/10.1007/978-981-16-2723-1_7

Table 1. Azure data configuration

Application type	CPU	Memory	Database	Network
General purpose	Low	Low	Low	Moderate
Compute optimized	High	High	Moderate	High
Memory optimized	Moderate	Low	Moderate	Low
Storage optimized	Low	Low	High	Low
High performance compute	Very high	High	High	Very high

is awfully difficult job for users to associate their QoS needs to configuration given by the provider. Migration from one provider to another is not only a risky process but also costly. This implies the significance of service selection framework. Application stack dependency or platform (Microsoft SQL) dependency occurs if the provisioning process implementation is not superlative. More technical problems faced to solve these challenges in cloud environment for its establishment. So, in near future cloud community not likely become reality while QoS requirements and available service configurations taken in to consideration.

A reliable service selection framework is needed for consumers to select best suitable (as per QoS) services. For this we proposed a novel fuzzy ANP framework which considers individual customer's QoS criteria based service selection. Even though huge research models and frameworks exists for making best selection of services, many of those approaches could not capture the QoS information and lack of validation. Hence, the existing methods are prejudiced with the uncertainty in information given by cloud providers, ambiguous specification of requirements by consumer and also fictitious estimation of QoS [4] based on actual measurement on time and existing QoS of previous services. The proposed work can be organized as follows.

- Validating the specified service's configuration information by a third party validator.
- Actual measurement of QoS is taking by using monitoring tools.
- Taking into consideration, the customer reviews on performance of services in the provisioning process.
- The consumer's fuzzy estimation of Qos is simplified by designing Fuzzy ANP approach which is a Multi Criteria Decision Making Process.

The proposed framework can deal with indefinite consumer's requirements based on the QoS parameters.

2 Related Work

Different areas of research like virtualization, datacenter hardware design, software development, and resource provisioning are included in cloud computing. However, this paper [9] focuses on to improve the service selection [10] which is a part of re- source provisioning research [11].

Here, we mainly consider selection for IaaS services, which is a provider independent classification model [7]. Here, we compare and classify the cloud providers. From consumer's perspective, the main criteria behind IaaS provider's selection are determined by cloud provider's market analysis, international literature review and expert analysis. Gaurg et al. in [8], developed a software based framework which can automatically compute the quality attributes and hierarchize cloud services. The case study in this paper includes QoS parameters as well as cost, capacity and performance of customer's applications.

They proposed and used AHP based ranking algorithm to define key performance metrics of QoS parameters in SMI. But, they didn't consider exact customer's requirements. [22] introduced wide-ranging service QoS measurement Index (SMI) which consist of business related key performance indicators (KPIs) and this is a typical method for comparing and measuring service providers.

3 Fuzzy ANP Approach

For web based applications and SOA like grid computing [14] service selection has been introduced in many research works. So, more methods are available for solving the selection problem in others models [15]. A fuzzy cloud selection framework [13], proposed a model which consists of 4 modules (i) User Interface, (ii) Management of QoS component, (iii) Service Selection Module, and (iv) Cloud Service Repository component. We have customized the same model by using ANP (Analytical Network Process) as illustrated in Fig. 1. The existing model proposed by Tajvidhi et al. used AHP MCDM ranking algorithm, but it doesn't consider inter feedbacks of selection criteria.

Our proposed framework consists of 3 modules (i) User Interface, (ii) User feedback, and (iii) Cloud Service Repository as input sources for calculating the metrics. The first module called user interface collects the needed criteria and their relative important costs directly from consumers. This data may not be exactly concise, because the complexities and consumer's unclear perception of QoS parameters. Hence, a specific approach is defined as shown in Fig. 1. This is used for getting fuzzy based linguistic weights of criteria, and then the triangular fuzzy numbers are converted into simplified numbers, which can then be used in ranking algorithm called ANP.

This module consists of two other components (i) Metrics calculation and (ii) Ranking using ANP. The input for metric calculation is from two sources one is cloud service repository, which consists of data gathered from different sources and is published with a certification by third party vendor. This component's output is redirected to ranking algorithm called ANP which is shown in Fig. 2. At last the result will be displayed by user interface. For resolving this selection problem we should consider service attributes to be compared, make them comparable to choose a best structure.

3.1 QoS Management

In order to select the best service first we should select required service attributes and is a challenging task. This QoS management eases this task and is liable to model the most required criteria; QoS needs are mapped to available service configurations [13].

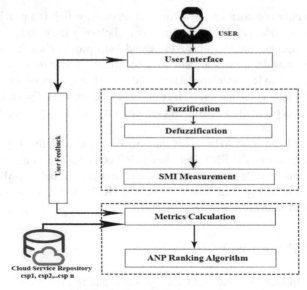

Fig. 1. Fuzz ANP framework

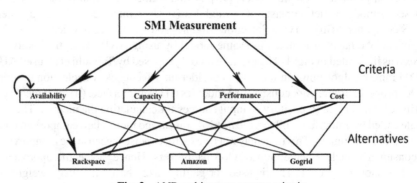

Fig. 2. ANP architecture among criteria

We need to choose one of the most appropriate model comparisons and service selection, because designing the QoS is trivial task for making optimal decisions in decision making systems [16]. To ease this task we have used the model SMI (Service Measurement Index) [4]. It is hierarchical view of service attributes that customer required in selection process [17].

3.2 Metrics Calculation

In proposed framework we consider AMI measurement. For many services, SMI approach is not available to define and capture QoS parameters dynamically [17, 18]. Service providers provide the service configuration statically. But they might not give accurate information due to competitive market. So, there is uncertainty in decision making. To handle this uncertainty, we have used cloud repository which has the cloud provider's data given in their own websites and it is maintained in a standard XML format. It is managed by cloud service broker [19], who is responsible for verifying the service provider's QoS violations to make data reliable.

During selection process, run time QoS attributes like reliability, performance etc. and past QoS performance considerations are another major issue. These run time QoS attributes information has not given by service providers [20]. In order to handle this, the best approach is user feedback, where the cloud consumers gave their live experiences. These cloud users information is more reliable than website information. This component is introduced based on [21]. Hence, data is taken from two trustworthy sources; Cloud Service Repository and User Feedback.

4   Service Selection in Cloud Environment

To our proposed ANP-based [12] ranking method, criteria's comparative weight is one of the important inputs. It is given by fuzzy perception. Hence, first we describe fuzzy inference for getting comparative weights of the criteria and then describe the ANP algorithm used in this paper.

4.1   Fuzzy Logic

Cloud consumers give their weights by linguistic terms. Based on these terms we have to assign weight to each criterion by considering relative importance of the attribute. Then fuzzy sets convert these into simplified numbers.

Triangular Weight Matrix: Cloud users are giving their requirements and constraints as weights for each criterion as shown in Table 1 using linguistic terminology. Because these terms cannot be used in ANP algorithm, as it requires weights in numerals. Hence we used Defuzzification, in order to get the simplified numbers. So, each term is allocated with the triangular fuzzy numbers, suppose if customer chooses criterion called more important, its corresponding fuzzy set is (5, 7, 9) as shown in Table 2.

Table. 2. Triangular fuzzy numbers of linguistic terms

Linguistic terms	Triangular fuzzy number
Not important	(1, 1, 1)
Less important	(1, 3, 5)
Definitely important	(3, 5, 7)
More important	(5, 7, 9)
Extremely important	(7, 9, 9)

Cost matrix is defined as shown in (1), where 'cap' symbol represents the triangular numbers.

$$A_i = \begin{pmatrix} d_{11} & \cdots & d_{1n} \\ \vdots & \ddots & \vdots \\ d_{m1} & \cdots & d_{mn} \end{pmatrix} \tag{1}$$

Cost matrix is defined as shown in (1), where 'cap' symbol represents the triangular numbers. The row of the matrix in (1) represents triangular numbers of all sub-criteria, i.e. d_{ij} denotes the significance of ith criterion and jth number.

Geometric Mean Calculation: Using [25] the geometric mean of sub criteria fuzzy value is calculated as defined in (2).

$$p_i = \left(\prod_{i=1}^{n} d_{ij} \right)^{1/n}, \ i = 1, 2, \ldots, n(n = 3) \tag{2}$$

Final fuzzy weight is defined as Final fuzzy weight is defined as

$$\hat{w}_i = \hat{p}_i \times (\hat{p}_1 + \hat{p}_2 + \ldots \hat{p}_n)^{-1} = (1w_i, mw_i, uw_i) \tag{3}$$

Defuzzification: To get non fuzzy numbers we need to defuzzify the above using center of area method [26] as follows:

$$df_i = \frac{1w_i + mw_i + um_i}{3} \tag{4}$$

We need to do normalization here as follows:

$$Nr_i = \frac{df_i}{\sum_{i=1}^{n} df_i} \tag{5}$$

These values are given as input to ANP ranking algorithm.

4.2 ANP Algorithm

Cloud consumers have given their requirements and constraints. ANP analyses and select the service which meets such requirements [12]. The ANP orders these chosen services based on their ranking procedure described in the following 3 steps.

- Solution for selection problem: It is specified in ranking objective (level 1), QoS attributes ordering with feedback (level 2) and cloud service providers like Rack-Space, Amazon EC2 and GoGrid (level 3).
- Pair wise comparison: Here, the relative importance of criteria over other criteria as well as with self can represented. Consider c_i and c_j be the values of criteria k for cloud services i and j respectively. Consider a_i and a_j be the cloud services then a_i/a_j, indicates the relative rank of a_i over a_j [3].

For each attributes, we calculated numeric and Boolean values differently by using proposed ranking method. Based on context, the numeric value has two types; those are in case of performance higher value is preferable where as in case of cost lower value is preferable. And if we consider higher value is better, then the value of specific QoS is a_i/a_j, or else a_j/a_i (if lower is better). The pairwise comparison matrices obtained as follows:

$$a_i/a_j = 1 \text{ if } a_i = a_j, \ a_i/a_j = w_k \text{ if } a_{i=1} \text{ and } a_{j=0}, a_i/a_j = 1/w_k \text{ if } a_0 = 0 \text{ and } a_j = 1 \quad (6)$$

- Aggregation of each criterion's relative importance: In this step, the relative ranking of matrices of each attribute are aggregated with their previous related weights. This process is repeated for all attributes which is helpful in ranking cloud services.

5 Example

Here, we use simple case study to implement this fuzzy ANP approach. The data regarding this QoS is collected from 3 IaaS cloud providers viz Rackspace [27], Amazon EC2 [28] and GoGrid [29]. In this example, we have considered few criteria for easy calculation as follows (i) Capacity, (ii) Cost and (iii) Performance. The data collected from official websites is shown in Table 3. Here, we explained the proposed fuzzy perception and ANP ranking method on real time data.

Table 3. QoS attributes for Azure, Amazon EC2 and GoGrid Cloud Services

First-level criteria	Second-level criteria	Value type	Microsoft azure	Amazon EC2	GoGrid
Capacity	CPU	Numeric	9.6	18.8	12.8
	Memory	Numeric	15	15	14
Cost	VM cost	Numeric	0.68	0.96	0.96
	Data (GB)	Numeric	10	10	8
	Storage	Numeric	12	15	15
Performance	Network availability	Numeric	99	99.99	100
	Urgent response	Boolean	0	1	1

5.1 Fuzzy Perception

Triangular Weight Matrix. Here, the input is taken from Table 4 and for each criterion the weight matrix is calculated based on (1). For first level criteria attribute called capacity

Table 4. QoS attributes for azure, amazon EC2 and GoGrid cloud services

First-level criteria	Second-level criteria	Importance	Triangular values	Geometric mean
Capacity	CPU	Extremely important	(7, 9, 9)	(4.6, 6.7, 7.9)
	Memory	Definitely important	(3, 5, 7)	
Cost	VM cost	Extremely important	(7, 9, 9)	(2.7, 5.12, 6.8)
	Data	Less important	(1, 3, 5)	
	Storage	Definitely important	(3, 5, 7)	
Performance	N/W availability	Extremely important	(7, 9, 9)	(2.6, 5.2, 6.7)
	Urgent response	Less important	(1, 3, 5)	

is calculated as matrix, here rows represent the sub criteria triangular numbers (CPU, Memory). So, the related matrix for capacity will be

$$\hat{V} = \begin{bmatrix} 7 & 7 & 9 \\ 3 & 5 & 7 \end{bmatrix} \tag{7}$$

For other criteria called cost with 3 sub criteria (VM cost, data, storage), the relative matrix is

$$\hat{C} = \begin{bmatrix} 7 & 9 & 9 \\ 1 & 3 & 5 \\ 3 & 5 & 7 \end{bmatrix} \tag{8}$$

Similarly, for performance, the relative matrix is

$$\hat{P} = \begin{bmatrix} 7 & 9 & 9 \\ 1 & 3 & 5 \end{bmatrix} \tag{9}$$

Calculating Geometric Mean. For each criterion the geometric mean based on (2) is as follows.

$$\hat{p}_1 = \left[(7*3)^{1/2}; (9*5)^{1/2}; (9*7)^{1/2} \right] \tag{10}$$

$$\hat{p}_2 = \left[(7*1*3)^{1/2}; (9*3*5)^{1/2}; (9*5*7)^{1/2} \right] \tag{11}$$

$$\hat{p}_3 = \left[(7*1)^{1/2}; (9*3)^{1/2}; (9*5)^{1/2} \right] \tag{12}$$

Table 5 shows geometric mean values of the available criteria. In addition to this, it also shows sum value and reverses value.

Calculating Fuzzy Value. By using sum and inverse of sum which is in last row of Table 5, fuzzy weight of capacity criteria is calculated based on (3) as follows

$$W1 = (4.6 * 0.1); \ (6.7 * 0.05); \ (7.9 * 0.04) = (0.46, 0.335, 0.316) \quad (13)$$

Similarly, other two criteria fuzzy weights are determined and shown in Table 5.

Defuzzyfication. Using center of area method (4) and normalization (5) we can defuzzify the value obtained in previous step as shown in Table 6. Attribute weights are required for ANP algorithm. Hence, we can use ANP algorithm in this context by considering each attribute's weight as matrix below

$$w_k = \begin{matrix} Capacity \\ Cost \\ Performance \end{matrix} \begin{bmatrix} 0.4 \\ 0.31 \\ 0.28 \end{bmatrix} \quad (14)$$

Table 5. Geometric mean

Criteria	$\hat{p}_i$		
Capacity	4.6	6.7	7.9
Cost	2.7	5.1	6.8
Performance	2.6	5.2	6.7
Sum	9.9	17.0	21.4
Reverse Sum	0.10	0.05	0.04

Table 6. Each criteria final fuzzy value

Criteria	W			df$_i$	Nr$_i$
Capacity	0.46	0.335	0.316	0.37	0.4
Cost	0.27	0.26	0.272	0.285	0.31
Performance	0.26	0.26	0.268	0.26	0.28

5.2 ANP Ranking Algorithm

1. *Design the problem as a network structure*: It is also like hierarchical structure but includes feedback with 3 first level criteria and 7 second level criteria as shown in Table 3.
2. *The pair wise comparison matrix*: Here, the comparison matrix for capacity attribute with sub criteria is calculated based on Table 1 as follows.

$$CM_{CPU} = \begin{matrix} Sp_1 \\ Sp_2 \\ Sp_3 \end{matrix} \begin{bmatrix} 1 & \frac{18.8}{9.6} & \frac{12.8}{9.6} \\ \frac{9.6}{18.8} & 1 & \frac{12.8}{18.8} \\ \frac{9.6}{12.8} & \frac{18.8}{12.8} & 1 \end{bmatrix} \quad (15)$$

Then the normalize vector for CPU and Memory capacity are:

$$nCM_{CPU} = \begin{bmatrix} 0.44 \\ 0.23 \\ 0.33 \end{bmatrix} \quad (16)$$

$$nCM_{Memory} = \begin{bmatrix} 0.33 \\ 0.33 \\ 0.32 \end{bmatrix} \tag{17}$$

By combining the above two we get the relative matrix for capacity attribute as follows:

$$RM_{Capacity} = \begin{bmatrix} 0.44 & 0.33 \\ 0.23 & 0.33 \\ 0.33 & 0.32 \end{bmatrix} \tag{18}$$

The normalized vector for this capacity is calculated as follows

$$nRM_{Capacity} = \begin{bmatrix} 0.38 \\ 0.29 \\ 0.32 \end{bmatrix} \tag{19}$$

Similarly, for cost and performance the resultant normalized matrices are as follows

$$nRM_{Cost} = \begin{bmatrix} 0.05 \\ 0.76 \\ 0.05 \end{bmatrix} \tag{20}$$

$$RM_{Performance} = \begin{bmatrix} 0.25 \\ 0.44 \\ 0.25 \end{bmatrix} \tag{21}$$

3. *Aggregating the relative importance of criteria*: To get the single matrix, we need to combine all the above relative matrices as follows:

$$\begin{bmatrix} 0.38 & 0.05 & 0.25 \\ 0.29 & 0.76 & 0.44 \\ 0.32 & 0.06 & 0.25 \end{bmatrix} \tag{22}$$

Now multiply this matrix with weights of QoS attributes which are calculated from fuzzy perception values (15)

$$\begin{bmatrix} 0.38 & 0.05 & 0.25 \\ 0.29 & 0.76 & 0.44 \\ 0.32 & 0.06 & 0.25 \end{bmatrix} \begin{bmatrix} 0.4 \\ 0.31 \\ 0.28 \end{bmatrix} = \begin{matrix} Sp_1 \\ Sp_2 \\ Sp_3 \end{matrix} \begin{bmatrix} 0.26 \\ 0.47 \\ 0.21 \end{bmatrix} \tag{23}$$

Hence the service providers are ranked as Sp2 > Sp1 > Sp3, Amazon EC2 (Sp2) got highest rank followed by Rack Space (Sp1) followed by GoGrid (Sp3).

6 Conclusion and Future Enhancement

Here, we proposed a cloud service selection approach called fuzzy ANP. The existing methods are not considering uncertainty of customer requirements. They only refer the data published by cloud service providers in their web sites and consumers vague conception of requirements. They also used AHP ranking algorithm [5] which is best for ranking services but it doesn't consider feedback among criteria. To get realistic QoS requirement, we have considered fuzzy perception of QoS and ranking the service providers using ANP algorithm which gives accurate results. We can also extend this for more QoS parameters to get better results which are applicable for real time scenario.

References

1. Hiran, K.K., et al.: Cloud Computing: Master the Concepts, Architecture and Applications with Real-world Examples and Case Studies, 1st edn. Kindle Edition
2. Wang, L., et al. (eds.): Cloud Computing: Methodology, Systems, and Applications. CRC Press, Boca Raton (2012)
3. Garg, S.K., Versteeg, S., Buyya, R.: Smicloud: a framework for comparing and ranking cloud services. In: 2011 Fourth IEEE International Conference on Utility and Cloud Computing (UCC). IEEE (2011)
4. Cloud Commons: Introducing the Service Measurement Index, Cloud Service Measurement Initiative Consortium (2012)
5. Tajvidi, M., et al.: Fuzzy cloud service framework. In: Proceedings of 2014 IEEE International Conference on Cloud Networking (CloudNet) (2014)
6. Vu, L.-H., Hauswirth, M., Aberer, K.: QoS-based service selection and ranking with trust and reputation management. In: Meersman, R., Tari, Z. (eds.) OTM 2005. LNCS, vol. 3760, pp. 466–483. Springer, Heidelberg (2005). https://doi.org/10.1007/11575771_30
7. Repschläger, J., et al.: Developing a Cloud Provider Selection Model. EMISA (2011)
8. Li, A., et al.: CloudCmp: comparing public cloud providers. In: Proceedings of the 10th ACM SIGCOMM Conference on Internet Measurement. ACM (2010)
9. Pawluk, P., et al.: Introducing STRATOS: a cloud broker service. In: 2012 IEEE 5th International Conference on Cloud Computing (CLOUD). IEEE (2012)
10. Hussain, F.K., Omar, K.H.: Towards multi-criteria cloud service selection. In: 2011 Fifth International Conference on Innovative Mobile and Internet Services in Ubiquitous Computing (IMIS). IEEE (2011)
11. Han, S.-M., et al.: Efficient service recommendation system for cloud computing market. In: Proceedings of the 2nd International Conference on Interaction Sciences: Information Technology, Culture and Human. ACM (2009)
12. Sumalatha, K., Bhanu, P.C.: Selection of architecture styles using analytic network process. Int. J. Commun. Eng. (IJCAE) 3(3), 07–15 (2012)
13. Dastjerdi, A.V., Buyya, R.: A taxonomy of QoS management and service selection methodologies for cloud computing. In: Wang, L., Ranjan, R., Chen, J., Benatallah, B. (eds.) Cloud Computing: Methodology, Systems, and Applications. CRC Press, Boca Raton (2011)
14. Al-Faifiab, A.M., Song, B.: Performance prediction model for cloud service selection from smart data. Future Gener. Comput. Syst. 85, 97–106 (2018)
15. Sun, L., Dong, H.: Cloud service selection: state-of-the-art and future research directions. J. Netw. Comput. Appl. 45, 134–150 (2014)
16. Whaiduzzaman, M., Gani, A.: cloud service selection using multi criteria decision analysis. Sci. World J. 2014, 10. Article ID 459375

17. Mu, B., Li, S., Yuan, S.: QoS-aware cloud service selection based on uncertain user preference. In: Miao, D., Pedrycz, W., Ślęzak, D., Peters, G., Hu, Q., Wang, R. (eds.) RSKT 2014. LNCS (LNAI), vol. 8818, pp. 589–600. Springer, Cham (2014). https://doi.org/10.1007/978-3-319-11740-9_54

18. Kumar, R.R., Kumar, C.: An evaluation system for cloud service selection using fuzzy AHP. In: 11th International Conference on Industrial and Information Systems (2016)

19. Kunhambu, D.V., Balan, R.V.S.: Efficient multi-objective particle swarm optimization based ranking system for cloud service selection. Inst. Eng. Technol. **13**(3), 297–304 (2019)

20. Wang, P.: QoS-aware web services selection with intuitionistic fuzzy set under consumer's vague perception. Expert Syst. Appl. **36**(3), 4460–4466 (2009)

21. Hussain, O.K., Parvin, S., Hussain, F.K.: A framework for user feedback based cloud service monitoring. In: 2012 Sixth International Conference on Complex, Intelligent and Software Intensive Systems (CISIS). IEEE (2012)

22. Kilincci, O., AslıOnal, S.: Fuzzy AHP approach for supplier selection in a washing machine company. Expert Syst. Appl. **38**(8), 9656–9664 (2011)

23. Fan, W., Yang, S.: A multi-dimensional trust-aware cloud service selection mechanism based on evidential reasoning approach. Int. J. Autom. Comput. **12**(2), 208–219 (2016). https://doi.org/10.1007/s11633-014-0840-3

24. Sumalatha, K., Anbarasi, M.S.: A review on various optimization techniques of resource provisioning in cloud computing. Int. J. Electr. Comput. Eng. (IJECE) **9**(1), 629–634 (2019). https://doi.org/10.11591/ijece.v9i1.pp.629-634. ISSN 2088-8708

25. Siegel, J., Perdue, J.: Cloud services measures for global use: the service measurement index (SMI). In: 2012 Annual SRII Global Conference (SRII). IEEE (2012)

26. Chou, S.-W., Chang, Y.-C.: The implementation factors that influence the ERP (enterprise resource planning) benefits. Decis. Support Syst. **46**(1), 149–157 (2008)

27. https://aws.amazon.com/ec2

28. https://www.rackspace.com/en-in

29. Ranjan, R., Benatallah, B.: Programming cloud resource orchestration framework: operations and research challenges. arXiv preprint arXiv:1204.2204 (2012)

Detecting Crisis Event on Twitter Using Combination of LSTM, CNN Model

Nayan Ranjan Paul[✉] and Rakesh Chandra Balabantaray

Department of Computer Science and Engineering, IIIT Bhubaneswar,
Bhubaneswar, Odisha, India
{c116008,rakesh}@iiit-bh.ac.in

Abstract. Twitter is being widely used as a preferred social media platform to report about many types of events to a larger audience, one such event is crisis event. People use Twitter to report these crisis and crisis related information during crisis situations such as natural and man-made disasters. Detecting these crisis events can improve situational awareness for general public, response agencies and aid agencies. Many works has done for crisis event detection which uses traditional machine learning techniques but very limited work has been reported which uses deep neural network. Deep neural network models have shown better results than standard machine learning models in recent years. Convolutional Neural Network (CNN) and Long Short-Term Memory (LSTM) are two such deep neural networks. CNN can recognize local features in a multidimensional field and LSTM network can learn sequential data as it has the ability of remembering previously read data. We are using two types of deep neural network called CNN-LSTM and LSTM-CNN in this paper, which is developed by combining both of CNN and LSTM networks for doing event detection during crisis situation on Twitter data. We provide the detailed explanation of both models and perform comparison against Support Vector Machine (SVM), CNN, and LSTM models. Our result shows that both models can successfully identify the presence of crisis related events accurately from twitter data. We find that LSTM-CNN model is the best achieving 8.7% better than regular SVM model.

Keywords: Event detection · Word embeddings · CNN · LSTM · LSTM-CNN · CNN-LSTM

1   Introduction

The increasing growth of communication technology in the form of social media has enabled millions of people to broadcast news and real world information about various events as they unfold on the ground. Among different types of social media platforms available today, one of the most popular platform is Twitter. Twitter has been extensively used as a valuable source of information

© Springer Nature Singapore Pte Ltd. 2021
P. K. Behera and P. C. Sethi (Eds.): CSI 2020, CCIS 1372, pp. 71–80, 2021.
https://doi.org/10.1007/978-981-16-2723-1_8

in various crisis situations such as floods, earthquakes [2], fire [3], cyclone, nuclear disaster [4].

Although actionable information is of greatest importance during the above mentioned crisis for providing timely help to those who are affected or going to be affected by these crisis, but to manually process such huge amount of twitter data during these crisis into meaningful, actionable, and sensible information is unfeasible for communities and different aid organizations [6]. Research has shown the importance of using twitter data in crisis situations. It has also shown that information spread through twitter can improve awareness in crisis situation for general public, response agencies and aid agencies.

There exist many works for event detection from twitter data which uses supervised and unsupervised machine learning models like language models, classifiers and clustering. Recently deep learning models have emerged as an important technique. Deep learning models provides significant improvement for various problems over traditional machine learning techniques. It is advantageous of using deep learning models because the model has the capacity to capture more than one layers of information. This motivates to use deep neural network model.

Our paper deals with the problem of detecting crisis events using deep learning methods on twitter data. So our goal is to use neural networks to detect crisis events. We use two different neural network models based on Sosa's model [7], that aim to merge the popular Long Short-Term Memory Neural Networks(LSTMs) with Convolutional Neural Networks (CNNs) and compare accuracy against regular CNN, LSTM and SVM models. The reminder of the paper is presented as follows. The next section provides background explanation of CNN and LSTM. Following that the scenario is presented. The model and experimental setup is discussed next. Before conclusion model comparison is presented.

2   Background

This section provides brief explanation about the Long Short-Term Memory (LSTM) recurrent neural network and Convolutional Neural Networks (CNN).

2.1   LSTM

Long Short-Term Memory (LSTM) is a special kind of recurrent neural network (RNN) utilized in the field of deep learning, which was proposed by Hochreiter and Schmidhuber. It is specifically designed to overcome the long-short term dependency problem, which remembers information for longer period in time. A typical LSTM memory block contains a forget gate, a cell, an input and output gate. The job of cell is to remember data over random intervals of time. The input, output and forget gates control information flow into and out of the cell. The input of new information to the memory is controlled by the input gate. The forget gate controls how long certain values are held in memory. The output gate regulates how much the value stored in memory affects the output activation of the block [8]. Figure 1 outline the details of an LSTM memory block and Eqs. 1 to 6 shows the mathematical formulation of every gate and cell state.

$$f_t = \sigma(W_f.[h_{t-1}, x_t] + b_f) \tag{1}$$

$$i_t = \sigma(W_i.[h_{t-1}, x_t] + b_i) \tag{2}$$

$$\tilde{C}_t = \tanh(W_C.[h_{t-1}, x_t] + b_C) \tag{3}$$

$$C_t = f_t * C_{t-1} + i_t * \tilde{C}_t \tag{4}$$

$$o_t = \sigma(W_o.[h_{t-1}, x_t] + b_o) \tag{5}$$

$$h_t = o_t * \tanh(\tilde{C}_t) \tag{6}$$

where weight matrix is W, bias term is b, tanh(.) and $\sigma(.)$ represents a hyperbolic tangent function and a sigmoid function respectively. In Fig. 1, x_t, and h_{t-1} are given as input to the four gates of the LSTM memory block named as f_t, i_t, o_t, $\tilde{c}_t$. Then the corresponding weights for forget, input and output gates are computed. A sigmoid activation function is used to calculate the values of those three gates, because the output of the function lies between zero and one both values inclusive. Depending on the output of the activation function the corresponding value will be kept (if the output is one) or entirely rejected (if the output is zero). To describe the amount of new information should be expressed in a cell state, a hyperbolic tangent function tanh is used. The information to be expressed in the cell state is determined by adding the result of point wise multiplication of forget gate value and the value of previous cell state with multiplying point wise the value of input gate and candidate value. Finally h_t, which is the output value of the LSTM memory block is calculated by multiplying

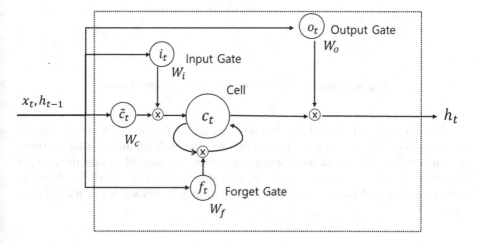

Fig. 1. Memory block of LSTM

point wise the value of output gate and the value calculated by applying tanh to the calculated value of cell state.

The benefit of using LSTM in text analysis is that, it can remember the previously read words which makes it better understanding of the inputs. For example lets take the following sentence "I thought there is an earthquake in Japan until I read the news paper." This sentence is not referring to the crisis situation but the first half of the sentence looks like it is related to an earthquake but the second half of the sentence changed it. LSTM can handle this type of changing perspective of the sentences.

2.2 CNN

A convolutional neural network (CNN) is a form of artificial neural network, that was initially used in area of image recognition but now it become an incredible model for various types of tasks. CNN can recognize local features in a multidimensional field.

Basic CNNs (as outlined in Fig. 2) take multidimensional data like word embeddings as input to a convolutional layer. The convolutional layer is composed of multiple filters which will learn different features by applying these filters sequentially to different sections of the input. The output is sub-sampled or pooled to smaller dimensions and later fed into a connected layer [9].

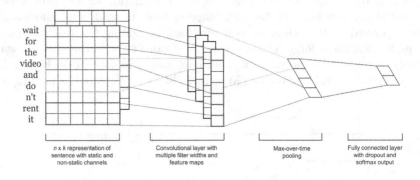

Fig. 2. Kim, Y. (2014). CNN for sentence classification

The idea behind using CNN is based on the fact that texts are structured and organised. We can expect that a CNN model can learn and predict patterns which may be lost through feed forward networks. For example it may distinguish the word "flood" in the context of "flood water in the city" which is related to a crisis as opposed to other sentence "flood of money" which is not related to a crisis.

3   Scenario

During crisis, people often use different social media platforms to post messages along with pictures of the crisis situations. Due to this millions of messages are appeared on these platforms. But among these messages many are not relevant or not informative. Olteanu et al. states that "crisis reports could be divided into three main categories of informativeness. They are related and informative, related but not informative and not related [10]". During the crisis, the meaningful and insightful social reports vary from 10% to 65% [11].

In this paper, we use the model based on sossa's model to efficiently identify the messages which are relevant. For this purpose, we consider the following task based on event types identified by [10].

– *Task - Messages related to crisis Vs Not related to crisis:* The aim of the task is to distinguish those tweets related to a crisis event from those tweets, which are not related to a crisis event.

4   Models

Detection of crisis events from tweeter data is a task of text classification with the aim of determining whether a given tweet represents a crisis or is linked to it. The CNN-LSTM and LSTM-CNN models are described in this section.

The model's pipeline contains of three main stages as follows

1. *Text preprocessing* - All the collected tweets of dataset are cleaned and tokenized for use in latter stages
2. *Word vector initialisation* - In this phase a word embedding matrix is created from a given pre-trained word embedding and a bag of words obtained from previous stage. This word embedding matrix will be used for training the model in next stage.
3. *CNN-LSTM and LSTM-CNN model training* - The word embedding matrix obtained from previous phase is used to train the models.

In the subsection below, we explain in more detail about each stage of the pipeline.

4.1   Text-Preprocessing

Tweets are generally contain noise, badly structured sentences, sometimes sentences are not complete because of the constant use of ill-formed words, irregular expressions, short forms, emojis, and words which are not present in dictionary. Therefore, to reduce tweets noise, this text-preprocessing phase applies a sequence of preprocessing steps on every tweet of the dataset. It includes removing of all URLs, emojis, the characters which are not English and not ASCII etc. After removing the noise from tweets, these tweets are then tokenized into word tokens and then these word tokens are given as input to the word vector initialisation stage.

4.2   Word Vector Initialisation

This phase initialized a word embedding matrix to train the classification models because it is essential to use word embedding for applying deep neural networks for text classification problem.

Word embedding is a name in which the words are represented in vectorized form with each word is mapped to a vector [12]. The key idea of using word embedding is that words with similar meaning should have a similar vector representation. Different methods for producing word embedding such as Word2Vec [13] and Glove [14] has been suggested in literature. In this work we choose Glove model to build word embedding matrix, in which rows of the matrix represents embedding vectors of the words in the Twitter dataset.

4.3   CNN-LSTM and LSTM-CNN Model Training

In this phase we train the CNN-LSTM and LSTM-CNN model from the word embedding matrix. The models are described below.

CNN-LSTM Model. The word embedding matrix obtained from the word vector initialization phase will be given as input to the initial convolution layer of the CNN-LSTM model. The convolution layer's output is taken as input by the max-pooling layer which pools the matrix to a smaller dimension, which in tern given as input into the LSTM layer. The concept behind this model is that the convolution layer extracts the local features and then the LSTM layer can use the ordering of these features to learn about the reordering of the input text. But this model is not quite as strong as the model of LSTM-CNN. The Fig. 3 shows the pipeline of the CNN-LSTM model.

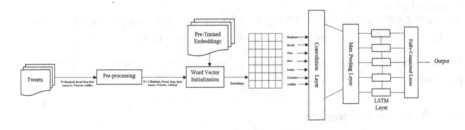

Fig. 3. Pipeline for the CNN-LSTM deep neural network event detection model.

LSTM-CNN Model. This model contains two layers of deep neural network, the first layer is an LSTM layer and the second layer is a CNN. The LSTM layer takes word embedding for each word in the tweet as input. The output vectors of this LSTM layer will store information for initial word as well as any previous words. Alternatively we can say that the LSTM layer is producing a new encoding of the original input. The output vectors of the LSTMs are concatenated to form a matrix and this matrix is then given as input to the convolution layer which is going to obtain local features. Finally, the convolution layer's output will be given as input to the max-pooling layer which in tern will be pooled to a smaller dimension and gives output as either crisis or not crisis related tweets. The Fig. 4 shows the pipeline of the LSTM-CNN model.

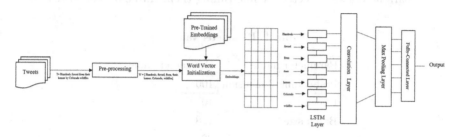

Fig. 4. Pipeline for the LSTM-CNN deep neural network event detection model.

5   Experimental Setup

The experimental setup is explained here, which is used to evaluate our event detection model. We are applying and testing the models on the task mentioned in Sect. 3. For this experiment we require to select a dataset and on that dataset evaluation will be done.

5.1   Twitter Dataset

To evaluate both model's performance, we need to use datasets where every tweet is annotated as to whether it is related to a crisis event or not. We use CrisisLexT26 dataset for this experiment and evaluation [15].

CrisisLexT26 dataset contains tweets gathered during twenty six crisis events in 2012 and 2013. This dataset contains tweets of which some are related to crisis and some are not. Each crisis includes about 1000 annotated tweets (some crisis contains more than 1000 tweets and some contains less than 1000 tweets) for total of 28000 tweets. Each tweet label showing whether a tweet is linked to a crisis event or not.

Out of these 28000 tweets we randomly selects 10000 tweets each for crisis related and unrelated tweets. So the dataset finally contains 20000 tweets where crisis related and non related number of tweets are same.

5.2 Evaluation

For the evaluation we divided the dataset with 16000 tweets for training which is 80% of total corpus and 4000 tweets for testing which is 20% of total corpus. These training and testing sets contained equal amount of crisis related and unrelated tweets. We have used tensorflow and keras API to create each of the five models. We trained each model using the parameters presented in Table 1 and we recorded the model's accuracy when trying to label the testing set.

The parameters are selected by fine tuning them through manual testing.

Table 1. Parameter values.

Parameter name	Parameter value
Embedding dimension	100
Epoch	10
Batch size	128
Filters	32
Kernel Size	3
Pool size	2
Dropout	.5
Word Enbeddings	Pre-Trained

6 Model Comparison

Here we present the results of our event detection models. Beside testing the CNN-LSTM and LSTM-CNN models, we also compare against standard CNN and LSTM networks. Furthermore we also compare with traditional SVM model with RBF kernels trained from word Unigrams as a baseline model because SVM is widely regarded as one of the best text classification model. The Table 2 shows the average accuracy of each event detection model taken after five tests.

Table 2. Average Accuracy of different models.

Model	Average accuracy
SVM	76.5%
CNN	77.2%
LSTM	82.6%
CNN-LSTM	80.3%
LSTM-CNN	85.2%

Result Analysis. All the deep learning models have higher accuracy than traditional SVM model. The CNN-LSTM model scored 3.1% higher in accuracy than the CNN model but 2.3% lower than the LSTM model. But the LSTM-CNN model scored 8% higher in accuracy than CNN model and 2.6% higher than LSTM model.

These results shows that our initial assumption was correct, that by combining CNN and LSTM, we are able to get both the CNN's ability in identifying local patterns and LSTM's ability to use the text's ordering. However the ordering of the layers is crucial.

It looks like that the convolutional layer of CNN-LSTM is unable to find some of the word's order or sequence information. That means if the convolutional layer does not provide any information, the LSTM layer will do nothing, it simply act as a fully connected layer. This model looks like, that it fail to make use of the full capabilities of LSTM layer and thus does not achieve its full potential. But on contrary, the LSTM-CNN model looks best because the first LSTM layer appears to be acting as an encoder so that there is an output token for each input token containing information not only for the original token, but also for all the previous tokens. Then using the richer representation of the original input, the CNN layer will be used to find the local patterns to enable better accuracy.

7 Conclusion

In this paper, we have used two models that combines LSTM and CNN neural networks to achieve better performance on crisis event detection which classify between crisis related and not related tweets. The model CNN-LSTM is doing 3.1% better than a regular CNN. The LSTM-CNN model, on the other hand, does 2.6% better than the LSTM model, and 8% better than the CNN. All the deep neural models perform better than traditional SVM model. For the future work we will be testing different types of RNNs for the model. For example we think that by using bidirectional LSTMs on the LSTM-CNN model might produce better result. Our future work also include to classify the tweets to detect the type of crisis and analyze the error and accuracy of detecting these crisis types.

References

1. Atefeh, F., Khreich, W.: A survey of techniques for event detection in Twitter. Comput. Intell. **31**(1), 132–164 (2015)
2. Qu, Y., Huang, C., Zhang, P., Zhang, J.: Microblogging after a major disaster in China: a case study of the 2010 Yushu earthquake. In: Proceedings of the ACM 2011 Conference on Computer Supported Cooperative Work, pp. 25–34. ACM (2011)
3. Vieweg, S., Hughes, A.L., Starbird, K., Palen, L.: Microblogging during two natural hazards events: what Twitter may contribute to situational awareness. In: Proceedings of the SIGCHI Conference on Human Factors in Computing Systems, pp. 1079–1088. ACM (2010)

4. Thomson, R., et al.: Trusting tweets: the Fukushima disaster and information source credibility on twitter. In: Proceedings of the 9th International ISCRAM Conference, pp. 1–10 (2012)
5. Zeng, Y., Yang, H., Feng, Y., Wang, Z., Zhao, D.: A convolution BiLSTM neural network model for Chinese event extraction. In: Lin, C.-Y., Xue, N., Zhao, D., Huang, X., Feng, Y. (eds.) ICCPOL/NLPCC -2016. LNCS (LNAI), vol. 10102, pp. 275–287. Springer, Cham (2016). https://doi.org/10.1007/978-3-319-50496-4_23
6. Gao, H., Barbier, G., Goolsby, R.: Harnessing the crowdsourcing power of social media for disaster relief. IEEE Intell. Syst. **26**(3), 10–14 (2011)
7. Sosa, P.M.: Twitter Sentiment Analysis using Combined LSTM-CNN Models, pp. 1–9 (2017)
8. Sundermeyer, M., Schlüter, R., Ney, H.: LSTM neural networks for language modeling. In: Interspeech, pp. 194–197 (2012)
9. Kim, Y.: Convolutional neural networks for sentence classification, arXiv preprint arXiv:1408.5882 (2014)
10. Olteanu, A., Vieweg, S., Castillo, C.: What to expect when the unexpected happens: social media communications across crises. In: Proceedings of the 18th ACM Conference on Computer Supported Cooperative Work & Social Computing, pp. 994–1009. ACM (2015)
11. Sinnappan, S., Farrell, C., Stewart, E.: Priceless tweets! A study on Twitter messages posted during crisis: black Saturday. In: ACIS 2010 Proceedings 39 (2010)
12. Bengio, Y., Ducharme, R., Vincent, P., Jauvin, C.: A neural probabilistic language model. J. Mach. Learn. Res. **3**(Feb), 1137–1155 (2003)
13. Mikolov, T., Chen, K., Corrado, G., Dean, J.: Efficient estimation of word representations in vector space. arXiv preprint arXiv:1301.3781 (2013)
14. Pennington, J., Socher, R., Manning, C.D.: Glove: global vectors for word representation. In: Empirical Methods in Natural Language Processing (EMNLP), pp. 1532–1543 (2014)
15. Olteanu, A., Castillo, C., Diaz, F., Vieweg, S.: CrisisLex: a lexicon for collecting and filtering microblogged communications in crises. In: ICWSM (2014)
16. Kim, T., Kim, H.Y.: Forecasting stock prices with a feature fusion LSTM-CNN model using different representations of the same data. PLOS One **14**(2) (2019). https://doi.org/10.1371/journal.pone.0212320

Implementation and Performance Analysis of FFT and Inverse FFT Using Openmp, MPI and Hybrid Programming on Virtual SMP/HPC Architecture

Jai G. Singla[✉] and Kirti Padia

Signal and Image Processing Group, Space Applications Centre, Indian Space Research Organization, Ahmedabad, India
{jaisingla,kirtipadia}@sac.isro.gov.in

Abstract. A Fast Fourier transform (FFT) algorithm computes the discrete Fourier transform (DFT) of a sequence, or it's inverse. Fourier analysis converts a signal from its original domain (often time or space) to a representation in the frequency domain and vice versa. An FFT rapidly computes such transformations by factorizing the DFT matrix into a product of sparse (mostly zero) factors. Fast Fourier transforms are widely used for many applications in engineering, science, and mathematics & signal and image processing. As, FFT remains a time consuming task on limited core machine and with a larger data set, we intended to implement this Fourier transformation technique on virtual SMP (HPC) with 144 CPU cores setup to improve the timings or to simultaneously handle multiple data sets. This paper consists of details about vSMP architecture designed by Scalemp [1], programming paradigms used, implementation details, performance and scalability analysis of Fast Fourier Transformation (FFT) on virtual Symmetric multiprocessor system (vSMP) using programming paradigms such as openMP, MPI and Hybrid programming, results and observations.

Keywords: VSMP · FFT · HPC · Optimization

1 Introduction

Fast Fourier transforms are widely used for many applications in engineering, science, and mathematics & signal and image processing. Image processing domain specially microwave image processing requires FFT computations at its core. Due to time consuming nature of this algorithm and volume of data, even parallel operations on workstation/server machine were not sufficient. To optimize and quickly process multiple datasets and reprocess entire acquisitions we analyzed usefulness of different programming paradigm for FFT processing. In further sections, we are explaining system architecture and HW details, parallel programming paradigm used, implementation details, performance and scalability analysis, observations and conclusions.

© Springer Nature Singapore Pte Ltd. 2021
P. K. Behera and P. C. Sethi (Eds.): CSI 2020, CCIS 1372, pp. 81–89, 2021.
https://doi.org/10.1007/978-981-16-2723-1_9

2 System Architecture and HW Details

Figure 1, contains the overall architecture diagram of virtual SMP designed by Scalemp [1]. There are in total 24 boards attached with Infiniband connectivity. Each or the board contains 4 CPU, 128 GB RAM, 16 HDD of 300GB each. Further, each CPU contains 6 cores. The system is managed through 1 GB network connectivity. Systems are aggregated through virtualized software layer [8]. In total, Aggregated Virtual SMP consists of 576 cores, 3 TB RAM and 88 TB of storage space. For the maximum utilization, the machine is reconfigured into four virtual machines, each with 144 cores each of 1.86 Ghz and 700 GB of RAM. System is based on Non uniform memory architecture (NUMA). The Target VM platform consists of 6 nodes each of 24 cores, total 144 cores; 128 GB RAM, total 700 GB and is interconnected using QDR infiniband.

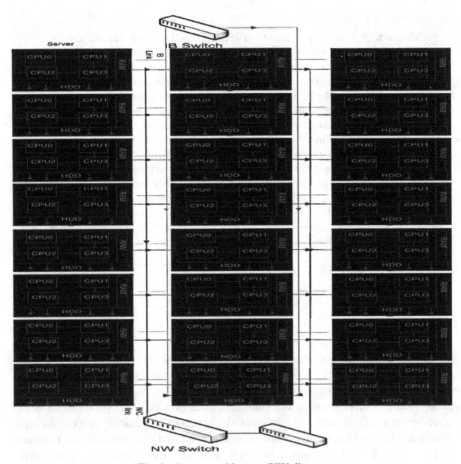

Fig. 1. System architecture/HW diagram

3 Programming Paradigm and Libraries Used

We analyzed the FFT performance on programming paradigms like openMP, MPI and Hybrid programming as per following details.

3.1 OpenMP

OpenMP is an Application Program Interface (API), jointly defined by a group of major computer hardware and software vendors [2]. OpenMP provides a portable, scalable model for developers of shared memory parallel applications. The API supports C/C++ and Fortran on a wide variety of architectures. We have used OpenMP compiler directives mainly for parallelization:

- Spawning a parallel region [2]
- Dividing blocks of code among threads [2]
- Distributing loop iterations between threads [2]
- Serializing sections of code [2]
- Synchronization of work among threads [2]

3.2 MPI

MPI is the first standardized, vendor independent, message passing library. The advantages of developing message passing software using MPI closely match the design goals of portability, efficiency, and flexibility [3]. MPI is not an IEEE or ISO standard, but has in fact, become the "industry standard" for writing message passing programs on HPC platforms [3]. This model demonstrates the following characteristics:

- A set of tasks that use their own local memory during computation. Multiple tasks can reside on the same physical machine and/or across an arbitrary number of machines [4].
- Tasks exchange data through communications by sending and receiving messages [4].
- Data transfer usually requires cooperative operations to be performed by each process. For example, a send operation must have a matching receive operation [4].

3.3 Hybrid (OpenMP + MPI)

Hybrid programming consists of MPI between the nodes and Shared memory programming inside of each node. It is a blend of OpenMP and MPI. When programmer wants to exploit the strengths of both models: the efficiency, memory savings, and ease of programming of the shared-memory model and the scalability of the distributed-memory model [7], hybrid model is the good option.

3.4 FFTW Library

FFTW [6] computes the DFT of complex data, real data, and even- or odd-symmetric real data. The input data can have arbitrary length [5]. FFTW employs O (n log n) algorithms for all lengths, including prime numbers [5].

4 Implementation Details

We have used openmp, MPI, hybrid programming and NUMA architecture knowledge for developing the routines. The developed routines can be used directly as an executable or through the developed scripts. Routines can be shared among the interested users as and when required.

4.1 Scenario1

To validate library settings, The FFT module and inverse FFT were calculated on single core & timing was noted.

Further, shared memory approach with openMP constructs was used. Using this approach, processing was limited largely to one board or one machine. For internode computations, with infiniband communications data was moved in and out of memory. So, this approach is best suited while doing parallel operations within the node.

The OpenMP routine can be invoked from command line by following arguments:

../exe/fft2hpc input_file $Nthreads out_file.

//This will invoke openmp version with specified no of threads.

4.2 Scenario2

In this approach, we performed FFT operations by using internode computation power. Message Passing Interfaces were used to move the data and get back the results. Data was move in and out using IB network. But, due to faster communications among various nodes, better scalability is expected in this scenario.

This MPI version can be invoked from command line by following arguments:

mpiexec -np $NPROC../exe/fft_mpi input_file out_file.

//This will invoke mpi routine with specified no of processes.

4.3 Scenario3

In this approach, we computed FFT operations using internode as well as intra-node compute power. So, openmp and MPI both were used. Here, as we are trying to utilize the capacity of the full machine, the best scalability is expected.

The hybrid routine can be invoked from command line by following arguments:

mpiexec -np $NPROC sh hybrid.sh $NThreads../exe/fft_mpi_thread input_file out_file.

//This will invoke hybrid routine with specified no of processes and threads.

To invoke kernel setting we have used scripts which can be used readily.

5 Performance Analysis and Scalability Analysis Results

Data set of size 8K × 18 K was taken to perform FFT and inverse FFT. Code was optimized using openMP, MPI and hybrid MPI programming models and middleware software kernel settings. The results are listed below:
Results with Input Image Size 8K × 18K

Table 1. Results with openMP

Serial no	Programming models	Execution units	Time	Speed X
1	Serial	Single core	54.9 s	1
2	openmp	4 cores	19.5 s	2.8
3	openmp	8 cores	14.5 s	3.8
4	openmp	16 cores	14.1 s	3.9
5	openmp	24 cores	13.8 s	4.0
6	ppenmp	32 cores	14.0 s	3.9

As seen in the Table 1, scalability is observed as we are increasing the no of cores (Tables 2, 3, 4, 5 and 6).

Table 2. Results with MPI

Serial no	Programming models	Execution units	Time	Speed X
1	Serial	Single core	54.9 s	1
2	MPI	4 P	30.8 s	1.8
3	MPI	8 P	22.0 s	2.5
4	MPI	16 P	14.6 s	3.8
5	MPI	32 P	13.0 s	4.22
6	MPI	48 P	13.9 s	3.94
7	MPI	64 P	15.5 s	3.54
8	MPI	128 P	25.4 s	2.16

Scalability is noted while increasing the cores from 1 to 64, when we are increasing the no of cores to 128, scalability is decreased as compared to 64 and 32 because of data movement overhead in message passing interface.

In case of hybrid approach, scalability is seen with increasing no of processes and threads.

Table 3. Results with hybrid programming

Serial no	Programming models	Execution units	Time	Speed X
1	Serial	single core	54.9 s	1
2	MPI + openmp	2 P, 24 cores	14.8 s	3.7
3	MPI + openmp	3 P, 24 cores	21.5 s	2.55
4	MPI + openmp	4 P, 24 cores	16.2 s	3.4
5	MPI + openmp	5 P, 24 cores	15.6 s	3.51
6	MPI + openmp	6 P, 24 cores	15.8 s	3.47

5.1 Results with Input Image Size 8K × 36 K

Further, the timings were obtained using bigger data set. Results are encouraging and similar trends have been observed in openmp, MPI and hybrid approach.

Table 4. Results with open MP

Serial no	Programming models	Execution units	Time	Speed X
1	Serial	Single core	110 s	1
2	openmp	4 cores	37 s	2.97
3	openmp	8 cores	26.0 s	4.23
4	openmp	16 cores	24.5 s	4.48
5	openmp	24 cores	24.8 s	4.43
6	openmp	32 cores	24.2 s	4.54

Table 5. Results with MPI

Serial no	Programming models	Execution Units	Time	Speed X
1	Serial	Single core	110 s	1
2	MPI	4 P	62.4 s	1.77
3	MPI	8 P	44.0 s	2.5
4	MPI	16 P	28.7 s	3.83
5	MPI	32 P	23.8 s	4.6
6	MPI	48 P	22.5 s	4.88
7	MPI	64 P	23.5 s	4.68
8	MPI	128 P	32.1 s	3.4

Table 6. Results with hybrid programming

Serial no	Programming models	Execution units	Time	Speed X
1	Serial	Single core	110 s	1
2	MPI + openmp	2 P, 24 cores	44.14 s	2.49
3	MPI + openmp	3 P, 24 cores	25.6 s	4.29
4	MPI + openmp	4 P, 24 cores	26.2 s	4.19
5	MPI + openmp	5 P, 24 cores	18.9 s	5.82
6	MPI + openmp	6 P, 24 cores	24.9 s	4.41

6 Observations

We have following observations on virtual SMP architecture: In case of OpenMP constructs, the program is very well behaved and provides very good performance and even scalability in case of low thread counts. However, from a certain thread count (which was 64), FFTW changes the way it distributes work to the threads. It starts assigning work in small chunks. Because of that, each cache line (which is 4KB in our case) will have data from many threads and if those threads are on multiple boards, the cache lines will be going back and forth between the boards. This slows down the performance in case of FFTW using openMP model and with no of threads >32.

In case of MPI model, when the data is shared among more than 64 processes, variation in the scalability is noted. The reason behind the same is the overhead involved in message passing among processes. So, if we have bigger datasets, more processes may produce optimum results. In case of hybrid model, results are moreover consistent.

There is fractional increase in code length that is 1–2% of entire code size while doing optimization. Programming paradigms used in this exercise can be used for windows environment also with comparable performance.

7 Validations

We took FFT of the input image and then inverse FFT of the same using all the above mentioned programming approaches. Input image and reproduced output results matches with a mean difference of 10^{-9}, which is acceptable in our scenario. Input image and reproduced output of FFT and inverse FFT are shown in Fig. 2 for visual validation.

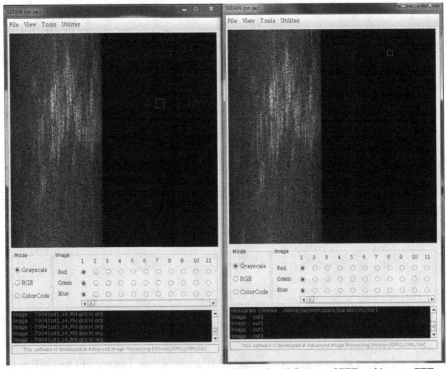

Input Image   Reproduced Output of FFT and inverse FFT

Fig. 2. Input & output validation

8 Conclusions

We have used FFTW library for calculating the FFT and inverse FFT operations because this is the fastest open source library available for FFT operations. We have obtained variation in timings with each of the programming paradigm. This does not lead to the conclusion that any one of this programming paradigm will always prove to be the best. But, in our case we got maximum speed up using hybrid programming paradigm where we had used openMP constructs within the server and MPI model among the servers. In Synthetic Aperture Radar (SAR) data processing, we are working in frequency domain and major time taking processes are Fourier transforms. Any improvement in timings of FFT and inverse FFT gives significant improvement in overall SAR data processing timings.

Acknowledgment. The authors express sincere gratitude to Shri. D. K. Das, Director, Space Applications Centre for permitting the presentation of this paper at the, CSI 53rd Annual convention to be held on 16-18th Jan, 2020 at Bhubaneswar. The authors are also grateful to Shri. N. M. Desai, Associate Director, Space Applications Centre for extending his support. Authors also thank then DD, SIPA, Shri Santanu Chowdhury for taking interest in this activity. Suggestions from internal referees to improve an earlier version of this paper are sincerely acknowledged.

References

1. ScaleMP web page. www.scalemp.com. Accessed 23 Dec 2019
2. Tutorials on OpenMP. https://computing/llnl.gov/tutorials/openMP. Accessed 23 Dec 2019. https://hpc.llnl.gov/openmp-tutorial
3. Tutorials on MPI. https://computing/llnl.gov/tutorials/mpi. Accessed 23 Dec 2019. https://hpc-tutorials.llnl.gov/mpi/
4. Tutorials on Parallel computing. https://computing/llnl.gov/tutorials/parallel_comp. Accessed 23 Dec 2019. https://hpc.llnl.gov/training/tutorials/introduction-parallel-computing-tutorial
5. Frigo, M., Johnson, S.G.: FFTW manual version 3.3.3, 25 November 2012
6. Frigo, M., Johnson, S.: The design and implementation of FFTW3. Proc. IEEE **93**, 216–231 (2005)
7. Lusk, E., Chan, A.: Early experiments with the OpenMP/MPI hybrid programming model. In: Eigenmann, R., de Supinski, B.R. (eds.) OpenMP in a New Era of Parallelism. IWOMP 2008. LNCS, vol. 5004, pp. 36–47. Springer, Heidelberg (2008). https://doi.org/10.1007/978-3-540-79561-2_4
8. White paper on The Versatile SMP™ (vSMP) Architecture and vSMP Foundation™ Aggregation Platform (2012)

Risk Preference Based Ranking of Suppliers Based on Interval Valued Trapezoidal Neutrosophic Number

Kiran Khatter[✉]

BML Munjal University, Gurgaon, India

Abstract. The paper presents a neutrosophic decision-making approach to select the suitable supplier among all the available supplier alternatives. In supply chain system, supplier selection is a significant decision to minimize the supply chain disruption risk. In practice, supplier is selected in unstructured way. There are many factors such as flexibility to meet urgent requirement, timely delivery, suitable price and good quality which must be considered in selecting the supplier. In this paper, all these factors are expressed in linguistic variables and weights are considered for each linguistic variable. These linguistic variables are further expressed in interval-valued-trapezoidal-neutrosophic-number. Then, interval-valued-trapezoidal-neutrosophic-weighted-arithmetic-averaging (IVTrNWAA) operator is used in multi-criteria-decision-making (MCDM) environment to solve supplier selection problem. Different levels of risk preference of expert are introduced to calculate the score values and accuracy degree, on the basis of which, all suppliers are ranked. The paper shows that it is important to consider the preference parameter/risk-attitude of decision maker and discusses how it affects the decision of supplier selection with the help of a case study on medical supply chain.

Keywords: Fuzzy Set (FS) · Intuitionistic Fuzzy Set (IFS) · Interval Valued Fuzzy Set (IVFS) · Interval Valued Intuitionistic Fuzzy Set (IVIFS) · Neutrosophic Set (NS) · Single Valued Neutrosophic Set (SVNS) · Trapezoidal Neutrosophic Set (TrNS) · Interval Valued Trapezoidal Neutrosophic Set (IVTrNS) · Interval Valued Trapezoidal Neutrosophic Number (IVTrNN) · Supply Chain Management · Medical Supply Chain · Multi-criteria Decision Making (MCDM)

1 Introduction

The objective of Supply Chain Management is to make sure that there is transparency of information amongst all the stakeholders such as manufacturers, suppliers, distributors, wholesalers and customers. Supply chain aims to ensure the timely delivery of products to distributors, wholesalers and customers by including a reliable and flexible supplier who can meet the requirements at the peak time. Supplier selection is very significant business problem for ensuring the competitiveness on the market. The problem with

© Springer Nature Singapore Pte Ltd. 2021
P. K. Behera and P. C. Sethi (Eds.): CSI 2020, CCIS 1372, pp. 90–99, 2021.
https://doi.org/10.1007/978-981-16-2723-1_10

supplier selection and determining procuremeft quotas from selected supplier is the most important phase for a manufacturer in the process of procurement of raw materials. In today's business environment, manufacturing companies can survive only if business process to select a supplier is efficient. Thus purchasing management is vital decision which affects the price of the product. In real life, we often come across the information which is incomplete, vague and uncertain and in such situations, it is not possible to take a determinate decision on the basis of incomplete information. Moreover, uncertainty is unavoidable in the information wherever decision is based on human judgement. Fuzzy set [1] was proposed to deal the vague, imprecise, uncertain and incomplete information with the help of membership degree. Later, IVFS was proposed [2] in case information is vague, uncertain, incomplete and imprecise but it is represented in interval. Afterwards, IFS [3] was presented to describe the grade of membership/non-membership. [4] generalized the IFS and introduced the triangular IFS (TIFS). Later on, [5] introduced IVIFS on the basis of IFS and IVFS to represent the fuzzy information in interval. [6] extended TIFS and introduced the trapezoidal-intuitionistic-fuzzy-set (TrIFS) to represent the membership and non-membership values of information which is trapezoid in nature. Since fuzzy set helps to deal with vague and uncertain information, many researchers [7–11] have proposed the fuzzy based approach to deal with supplier selection problem where supplier's effectiveness is based on multi criteria. Though fuzzy measures proposed by various researchers have been applied to solve this supplier selection problem, but degree of confidence of supplier in taking that decision was not be taken into account. If decision maker is not fully confident in taking a particular decision, effect of this indeterminacy should also be taken into consideration while taking a decision. Decision maker may be uncertain while making a decision but still gives a decision either in favor of acceptance or rejection. In such cases, it is not possible to represent the information by using only membership and non-membership functions for positive decision and negative decision respectively. Thus it is important to consider the uncertainty of expert while taking a decision. To handle such situations, [12] proposed the NS on the basis of FS and IFS; and introduced another membership function to determine the indeterminacy in addition to acceptance-membership and rejection-membership functions. Fuzzy-set considers only the membership for acceptance (truth) whereas IFS considers the membership for acceptance (truth) and membership for rejection (falsity). In case of NS, indeterminacy is considered as an independent element in addition to degree of truth and falsity membership [12]. Though in case of IFS, membership of indeterminacy can be computed by using truth and falsity membership but it was not considered as an independent element. Later on, concept of SVNS was introduced to use neutrosophic sets in real world scenario [13]. [14] extended the concept of SVNS and trapezoidal fuzzy numbers (TrFN) and proposed TrNS to deal with information which is neutrosophic and trapezoidal in nature.

Later on, interval valued trapezoidal neutrosophic set was introduced in [15] to represent trapezoidal neutrosophic information which is in some range/interval. A methodology was also proposed to deal with multi-attribute problems where information is trapezoidal neutrosophic/triangle neutrosophic and is in the form of interval [15]. But in

[15], risk-attitude of decision maker was not taken into account to deal with the multi-criteria problems. The paper extends the approach proposed by [15] and incorporate the risk-preference of expert while taking a decision in MCDM environment.

2 Preliminaries

2.1 Fuzzy Set

Since in mathematical modeling, we don't take uncertainty, human judgement capability and impreciseness into account while taking a decision. And in computer Programming, we use Boolean logic to make a decision. But in real life, we take decision with the help of linguistic words such as very good, good, bad, excellent, high or very high. Considering this human tendency to use linguistic words, Zadeh [1] proposed fuzzy set to manage vague, incomplete, imprecise and uncertain information which is represented linguistically such as highly reliable, low flexible, low performance etc. [16].

Definition: A fuzzy-set F in universe U is a defined as $F = \{\langle u, \mu_F(u) \rangle : u \in U\}$ where every element of U is mapped to $[0, 1]$ by $\mu_F : U \to [0, 1]$. This set considers only single value $\mu_F(u) \in [0, 1]$ to represent the degree of membership for F on A. As a result, degree of non-membership can be determined by $1 - \mu_F(u)$. The membership function helps to view the fuzzy information graphically. Different fuzzy sets are proposed by [1] for different type of membership function such as Singleton, L Function, Triangular etc. The triangular membership function is defined by a value $s1$ which lies between $r1$ and $t1$ ($r1 < s1 < t1$) as given below:

$$\mu_F(u) = \begin{cases} \frac{u-r1}{s1-r1} & r1 < u < s1 \\ 1 & u = s1 \\ \frac{t1-u}{t1-s1} & s1 < u < t1 \\ 0 & u \geq t1, u \leq r1 \end{cases} \tag{1}$$

2.2 IVFS

In real world scenario, sometimes it is not possible to exactly represent the opinion by some real value. As fuzzy set uses only single value for membership degree of information, in that case fuzzy set cannot be an appropriate choice. In order to represent uncertainty in membership of information, Zadeh [2] introduced IVFS where an interval is used to represent the membership of fuzzy information. Let $F = [w^-, w^+], w^-, w^+ \in [0, 1], w^- \leq w^+$ then $F : U \to [0, 1]$ is known as IVFS [17].

2.3 IFS and IVIFS

In some situations, where information is incomplete and uncertain, it is important to take into account both the acceptance (truth) membership and rejection (falsity) membership degree which was not the case with fuzzy set. [2] introduced IFS to represent the degree of acceptance and degree of rejection in information. An IFS F in universe U is represented as $F = \{\langle u, \mu_F(u), v_F(u)\rangle : u \in U\}$ where $0 \leq \mu_F(u) + v_F(u) \leq 1$. The function $\mu_F : U \rightarrow [0, 1]$ signifies the truth-membership degree of a whereas $v_F : U \rightarrow [0, 1]$ signifies degree of rejection (falsity) membership of a. Though, degree of indeterminacy can be determined as $1 - \mu_F(u) - v_F(u)$ [18]. In case of IVIFS, $\mu_F(u)$ represents values in interval for degree of membership such that $\mu_F(u) = [\mu_F^-(u), \mu_F^+(u)]$ and $v_F(u)$ represents values in interval for degree of non-membership such that $v_F(u) = [v_F^-(u), v_F^+(u)]$ with the condition $0 \leq \mu_F^+(u) + v_F^+(u) \leq 1$.

2.4 NS/SVNS

[12] introduced the concept of neutrosophic-set (NS) which considers inability of expert in taking a decision and introduces the degree of unknowingness/indeterminacy in addition to degree of acceptance i.e. truth-membership and degree of rejection i.e. falsity-membership. A neutrosophic set P in universe U is described as $P = \{\langle u, T_P(u), I_P(u), F_P(u)\rangle : u \in U\}$ where $T_P(u) + I_P(u) + F_P(u) \in]^-0, 1^+[$. T_P symbolizes the degree of acceptance of element u in set P such that $T_P : U \rightarrow]^-0, 1^+[$, I_P symbolizes the degree of unknowingness of element u in set P such that $I_P : U \rightarrow]^-0, 1^+[$ and F_P represents the degree of rejection $F_P : U \rightarrow]^-0, 1^+[$ is such a way that $^-0 \leq \sup T_P(u) + \sup I_P(u) + \sup F_P(u) \leq 3^+$. Since NS cannot be used in solving engineering problems because it takes values from interval $]^-0, 1^+[$. Later, [13] proposed SVNS in which all the membership functions (acceptance, unknowingness and rejection) consider from interval $[0, 1]$. A SVNS P in U is defined as $P = \{\langle u, T_P(u), I_P(u), F_P(u)\rangle : u \in U\}$ such that $T_P(u), I_P(u)$ and $F_P(u) \in [0, 1]$.

2.5 Interval Valued Trapezoidal Neutrosophic Set (IVTrNS)

Khatter K. [15] introduced the concept of interval-valued-trapezoidal-neutrosophic-set (IVTrNS) where all the (acceptance, unknowingness and rejection) membership functions are defined in some interval. Let $\tilde{\tilde{S}}$ is IVTrNS on universe U is defined by $\tilde{\tilde{S}}(u) = \tilde{\tilde{S}}^-(u), \tilde{\tilde{S}}^+(u)$, where $\tilde{\tilde{S}}^-$ and $\tilde{\tilde{S}}^+$ are lower and upper TrNS of $\tilde{\tilde{S}}$ such that $\tilde{\tilde{S}}^- \subseteq \tilde{\tilde{S}}^+$. $\tilde{\tilde{S}}^- = \left\{\langle u, T_{\tilde{S}}^-(u), I_{\tilde{S}}^-(u), F_{\tilde{S}}^-(u)\rangle : u \in U\right\}$ is lower TrNS where $T_{\tilde{S}}^-(u) \subset [0, 1]$ represents lower degree of acceptance-membership for trapezoidal-neutrosophic-number(TrNN) (a^-, b^-, c^-, d^-), $I_{\tilde{S}}^-(u) \subset [0, 1]$ represents lower degree of unknowingness for TrNN (e^-, f^-, g^-, h^-) and $F_{\tilde{S}}^-(u) \subset [0, 1]$ represents lower degree of rejection for TrNN (l^-, m^-, n^-, p^-) with the condition $0 \leq T_{\tilde{S}}^-(u) + I_{\tilde{S}}^-(u) + F_{\tilde{S}}^-(u) \leq 3$.

$\tilde{\tilde{S}}^+ = \left\{\langle u, T_{\tilde{S}}^+(u), I_{\tilde{S}}^+(u), F_{\tilde{S}}^+(u)\rangle : u \in U\right\}$ is upper TrNS where $T_{\tilde{S}}^+(u) \subset [0, 1]$ represents upper degree of acceptance for TrNN (a^+, b^+, c^+, d^+), $I_{\tilde{S}}^+(u) \subset [0, 1]$ represents upper degree of unknowingness for TrNN (e^+, f^+, g^+, h^+) and $F_{\tilde{S}}^+(u) \subset [0, 1]$ represents upper degree of rejection for TrNN (l^+, m^+, n^+, p^+) with condition $0 \leq T_{\tilde{S}}^+(u) + I_{\tilde{S}}^+(u) + F_{\tilde{S}}^+(u) \leq 3$.

Khatter K. [15] also proposed interval-valued-trapezoidal-neutrosophic-weighted-arithmetic-averaging (IVTrNWAA) operator to deal problems in the multi-criteria decision making (MCDM) environment as follows:

$$IVTrNWAA(\tilde{s}_1, \tilde{s}_2, \ldots, \tilde{s}_n) = w_1\tilde{s}_1 \oplus w_2\tilde{s}_2 \oplus w_3\tilde{s}_3 \oplus \cdots \oplus w_n\tilde{s}_n = \overset{n}{\underset{j=1}{\oplus}}(w_j\tilde{s}_j)$$

$$= \left\langle \left[\begin{pmatrix} 1 - \prod_{j=1}^{n}\left(1 - a_j^{-}\right)^{w_j}, 1 - \prod_{j=1}^{n}\left(1 - b_j^{-}\right)^{w_j}, \\ 1 - \prod_{j=1}^{n}\left(1 - c_j^{-}\right)^{w_j}, 1 - \prod_{j=1}^{n}\left(1 - d_j^{-}\right)^{w_j} \end{pmatrix}, \begin{pmatrix} 1 - \prod_{j=1}^{n}\left(1 - a_j^{+}\right)^{w_j}, 1 - \prod_{j=1}^{n}\left(1 - b_j^{+}\right)^{w_j}, \\ 1 - \prod_{j=1}^{n}\left(1 - c_j^{+}\right)^{w_j}, 1 - \prod_{j=1}^{n}\left(1 - d_j^{+}\right)^{w_j} \end{pmatrix} \right], \right.$$

$$\left. \left[\begin{pmatrix} \prod_{j=1}^{n} e_j^{-w_j} \prod_{j=1}^{n} f_j^{-w_j} \prod_{j=1}^{n} g_j^{-w_j} \prod_{j=1}^{n} h_j^{-w_j} \end{pmatrix}, \begin{pmatrix} \prod_{j=1}^{n} e_j^{+w_j} \prod_{j=1}^{n} f_j^{+w_j} \prod_{j=1}^{n} g_j^{+w_j} \prod_{j=1}^{n} h_j^{+w_j} \end{pmatrix}, \begin{pmatrix} \prod_{j=1}^{n} l_j^{-w_j} \prod_{j=1}^{n} m_j^{-w_j} \prod_{j=1}^{n} n_j^{-w_j} \prod_{j=1}^{n} p_j^{-w_j} \end{pmatrix}, \begin{pmatrix} \prod_{j=1}^{n} l_j^{+w_j} \prod_{j=1}^{n} m_j^{+w_j} \prod_{j=1}^{n} n_j^{+w_j} \prod_{j=1}^{n} p_j^{+w_j} \end{pmatrix} \right] \right\rangle \quad (2)$$

where $w_j (j = 1, 2, 3, \cdots, n)$ is weight of IVTrNN $\tilde{s}_j (j = 1, 2, 3, \cdots, n)$ with $w_j \in [0, 1]$ and $\sum_{j=1}^{n} w_j = 1$.

3   Supplier Selection Problem in Medical Supply Chain

High health expenses, increase in number of healthcare service providers (hospitals, clinics, nursing homes, health centres) and quality requires effective medical supply chain to use all the resources efficiently. A case study is presented on medical supply chain in which it is tough to track the supply of medicine/equipment in real time at each stage of supply chain. This will raise the cost as well as affects the relation with customer as well [19]. The healthcare service providers include facilities such as ICU, operation theatre, clinical laboratories, and emergency services. Generally, purchase department of service, providers considers only three major supplier selection criteria such as cost of medical supply/equipment, quality of supply/equipment and time of delivery to evaluate supplier. There always had been pressure on health care services to optimize the process of purchasing in order to get medical supply at the time when it is needed. After the discussion held with the panel of 6 experts, the attributes identified various key factors which helps in evaluating the medical supplier such as price of medical supply/equipment, quality of medical supply/equipment, conformity of medical supply/equipment, responsiveness to meet demand at peak and emergency hours, time of delivery, payment dealing, reliability, experience in medical supply, service quality and safety of medical supply. The experts are asked to give opinions on the importance of each supplier alternative and they expressed their opinions about each criteria using linguistic words such as very-low (VL), low (L), moderate (M), high (H) and very-high (VH). The experts conceived the criteria for each supplier alternative in terms of interval of TrNNs as given below in Table 1:

Table 1. Linguistic variables defined by expert (Trapezoidal-Neutrosophic-Number)

Linguistic meaning	Trapezoidal neutrosophic number
Very-Low	$((0.1, 0.1, 0.1, 0.2), (0.1, 0.1, 0.1, 0.1), (0.5, 0.5, 0.6, 0.7))$
Low	$((0.1, 0.3, 0.2, 0.5), (0.0, 0.1, 0.2, 0.3), (0, 0.1, 0.2, 0.2))$
Moderate	$((0.3, 0.4, 0.4, 0.3), (0.3, 0.3, 0.3, 0.3), (0.1, 0.1, 0.3, 0.3))$
High	$((0.3, 0.5, 0.6, 0.7), (0.2, 0.1, 0.3, 0.3), (0.1, 0.2, 0.3, 0.1))$
Very-High	$((0.7, 0.8, 0.7, 0.6), (0.1, 0.1, 0.2, 0.3), (0.1, 0.1, 0.1, 0.1))$

Then, expert defined the interval decision matrix as represented in Table 2.

[15] proposed an approach to resolve multi-criteria-decision-making problems dealing with neutrosophic and trapezoidal information which is represented in some interval but did not consider the attitude of decision maker towards supplier selection. In this study, attitude of decision maker towards supplier selection is taken into account whether decision maker is neutral, risk taker or risk aversive. Considering the fact that experts always strive to increase truth-degree, and decrease indeterminacy/falsity degree of information, following score and accuracy functions for IVTrNN $\left(\tilde{\tilde{s}}\right)$ are proposed keeping in mind the risk-preference of decision maker (λ):

$$Score\left(\tilde{\tilde{s}}\right) = \tfrac{1}{6}\Big[4 + \lambda\Big(\tfrac{a^-+b^-+c^-+d^-}{4} + \tfrac{a^++b^++c^++d^+}{4}\Big)$$
$$- (1-\lambda)\Big(\tfrac{e^-+f^-+g^-+h^-}{4} + \tfrac{e^++f^++g^++h^+}{4}\Big)$$
$$- (1-\lambda)\Big(\tfrac{l^-+m^-+n^-+p^-}{4} + \tfrac{l^++m^++n^++p^+}{4}\Big)\Big], Score \in [0, 1] \qquad (3)$$

$$Accuracy = \tfrac{1}{2}\Big[\lambda\Big(\tfrac{a^-+b^-+c^-+d^-}{4} + \tfrac{a^++b^++c^++d^+}{4}\Big)$$
$$- (1-\lambda)\Big(\tfrac{l^-+m^-+n^-+p^-}{4} + \tfrac{l^++m^++n^++p^+}{4}\Big)\Big], Accuracy \in [-1, 1] \qquad (4)$$

Table 2. Decision matrix in the form of interval

	SA1	SA2	SA3	SA4	SA5
Price of medical supply/equipment (C_1)	[Low, High]	[Very-Low, High]	[Very-Low, High]	[Medium, High]	[Low, High]
Quality of medical supply/equipment (C_1)	[Very-Low, High]	[Medium, High]	[Low, High]	[Medium, High]	[Low, High]
Responsiveness to meet demand at peak and emergency hours (C_3)	[Very-Low, Very-High]	[Very-low, High]	[Very-low, High]	[Very-low, High]	[Very-low, Very-High]
Time of delivery (C_4)	[High, Very-High]	[Medium, High]	[High, Very-High]	[Medium, Very-High]	[High, Very-High]
Payment dealing (C_5)	[Low, High]	[High, Very-High]	[Very-low, High]	[Medium, Very-High]	[Very-low, High]

where higher the value of $Accuracy\left(\tilde{\tilde{s}}\right)$, larger the value of accuracy of IVTrNN $\tilde{\tilde{s}}$.

IVTrNNs ($\tilde{\tilde{s}}_1$ and $\tilde{\tilde{s}}_2$) can be compared using score functions in such a way that if $Score\left(\tilde{\tilde{s}}_1\right)$ is greater than $Score\left(\tilde{\tilde{s}}_2\right)$, then $\tilde{\tilde{s}}_1 > \tilde{\tilde{s}}_2$. If score of $\tilde{\tilde{s}}_1 =$ score of $\tilde{\tilde{s}}_2$, then accuracy function is used for comparison. If $Accuracy\left(\tilde{\tilde{s}}_1\right) > Accuracy\left(\tilde{\tilde{s}}_2\right)$, then $\tilde{\tilde{s}}_1 > \tilde{\tilde{s}}_2$. If accuracy of $\tilde{\tilde{s}}_1 =$ accuracy of $\tilde{\tilde{s}}_2$, then $\tilde{\tilde{s}}_1 = \tilde{\tilde{s}}_2$. λ represents risk attitude and ranges from 0 to 1 as follows: If $\lambda \in [0, 0.5)$, decision-maker is risk taker and consider uncertainty about the factor affecting supplier decision, If $\lambda = 0.5$, decision-maker is neutral about factor affecting supplier decision, If $\lambda \in (0.5, 1]$, expert avoids taking risk while deciding about the factor affecting supplier selection and gives preference to certainty.

Suppose A is a set of supplier alternatives $A = (SA_1, SA_2, SA_3, \ldots, SA_n)$ satisfying a set of criteria $C = (C_1, C_2, C_3, \ldots, C_n)$. The experts assesses each alternative based on the specified criteria in the form of interval-valued-trapezoidal-neutrosophic-decision matrix [15]:

$$D = \left(\tilde{\tilde{d}}_{ij}\right)_{m \times n} = \begin{pmatrix} \langle[(a_{ij}^-, b_{ij}^-, c_{ij}^-, d_{ij}^-), (a_{ij}^+, b_{ij}^+, c_{ij}^+, d_{ij}^+)]\rangle, \\ \langle[(e_{ij}^-, f_{ij}^-, g_{ij}^-, h_{ij}^-), (e_{ij}^+, f_{ij}^+, g_{ij}^+, h_{ij}^+)]\rangle, \\ \langle[(l_{ij}^-, m_{ij}^-, n_{ij}^-, p_{ij}^-), (l_{ij}^+, m_{ij}^+, n_{ij}^+, p_{ij}^+)]\rangle \end{pmatrix}_{m \times n} \tag{5}$$

where

$(a^-, b^-, c^-, d^-) \subset [0, 1]$ and $(a^+, b^+, c^+, d^+) \subset [0, 1]$ represents lower degree and upper degree in favor of satisfaction of criteria C_i about the supplier alternative SA_j;

$(e^-, f^-, g^-, h^-) \subset [0, 1]$ and $(e^+, f^+, g^+, h^+) \subset [0, 1]$ represents lower degree and upper degree of ignorance about the criteria C_i for supplier alternative SA_j;

$(l^-, m^-, n^-, p^-) \subset [0, 1]$ and $(l^+, m^+, n^+, p^+) \subset [0, 1]$ represents lower degree and upper degree of satisfaction of criteria C_i about supplier alternative SA_j;

Some decision makers may give more importance to SA_3 alternative in comparison to SA_5 whereas for some other experts, SA_5 may be preferred alternative to go ahead. Weight vector of decision maker for supplier alternatives is assumed as $Weight = (0.2, 0.2, 0.25, 0.25, 0.2)^T$. $Score(\tilde{d}_i)(i = 1, 2, 3, 4, 5)$ is calculated to rank supplier the alternatives $SA_i(i = 1, 2, 3, 4, 5)$ as shown in Table 3 considering that decision-maker is risk taker, neutral or risk aversive while taking a decision:

Table 3. Score of supplier alternatives for different risk attitudes

SA_i	λ (Risk attitude of decision maker)										
	0	0.1	0.2	0.3	0.4	0.5	0.6	0.7	0.8	0.9	1
	$Score(\tilde{d}_i)(i = 1, 2, 3, 4, 5)$										
SA_1	0.570	0.593	0.617	0.640	0.663	0.686	0.710	0.733	0.756	0.780	0.803
SA_2	0.560	0.587	0.613	0.639	0.666	0.692	0.718	0.744	0.771	0.797	0.823
SA_3	0.575	0.600	0.624	0.649	0.674	0.698	0.723	0.748	0.772	0.797	0.822
SA_4	0.565	0.596	0.626	0.656	0.687	0.717	0.747	0.778	0.808	0.838	0.869
SA_5	0.583	0.610	0.636	0.663	0.689	0.716	0.742	0.769	0.795	0.822	0.848
Ranking	SA5 > SA3 > SA1 > SA4 > SA2	SA5 > SA3 > SA4 > SA1 > SA2	SA5 > SA4 > SA3 > SA1 > SA2	SA5 > SA4 > SA3 > SA1 > SA2	SA5 > SA4 > SA3 > SA1 > SA2	SA4 > SA5 > SA3 > SA2 > SA1	SA4 > SA5 > SA3 > SA2 > SA1	SA4 > SA5 > SA3 > SA2 > SA1	SA4 > SA5 > SA3 > SA2 > SA1	SA4 > SA5 > SA3 > SA2 > SA1	SA4 > SA5 > SA2 > SA3 > SA1

Table 3 shows that effect of different risk attitudes on the ranking of supplier selection. For risk taker, Supplier SA_5 is preferred supplier for purchasing medical supply but for risk aversive decision maker, SA_4 is the desirable supplier to get the medical supply.

It is evident from the Table 3, if $\lambda = 0$, decision-maker is taking risk and considers uncertainty into account. His *score* s for each supplier is based on the information on indeterminacy and falsity component. If $\lambda = 0.05$, decision-maker is neutral in taking a decision.. if $\lambda = 1$, decision-maker is risk aversive and his *score* s for each supplier is based on the facts favorable to the supplier and excludes the indeterminacy and falsity component. Thus proposed approach provides various solutions to supplier selection problem with various degree of risk attitude, represented by λ, where information is imprecise, incomplete, vague and indeterminate. This way, decision-maker will have enough information about the ranking of supplier alternatives from different perspectives and can weigh all the possible solutions to take suitable decision.

The paper extended the methodology proposed by [15] to handle MCDM problems where information is trapezoidal neutrosophic and is in interval of real numbers while considering the fact that human judgement is subjective. The method proposed in the paper considers risk-preference of decision-maker which was missing in [15].

4 Conclusion

In this paper, an approach is proposed to solve multi-criteria decision-making problems (MCDM) considering the fact that experts have different tendency to take risk. The risk preference of expert is introduced ranging from high risk (0) to low risk (1) in solving MCDM problems. Considering the indeterminacy component of IVTrNNs, experts always try to maximize the degree of acceptance, minimize the degree of unknowingness and rejection; score and accuracy are proposed according to different risk-attitudes of experts. A case study on medical supply chain is presented to illustrate the relevance of the developed method.

References

1. Zadeh, L.A.: Fuzzy sets. Inf. Control **8**(5), 338–353 (1965)
2. Zadeh, L.: The concept of a linguistic variable and its application to approximate reasoning(I). Inf. Sci. **8**, 199–249 (1975)
3. Atanassov, K.T.: Intuitionistic fuzzy sets. Fuzzy Sets Syst. **20**(1), 87–96 (1986)
4. Liu, F., Yuan, X.H.: Fuzzy number intuitionistic fuzzy set. Fuzzy Syst. Math. **21**(1), 88–91 [12] (2007)
5. Atanassov, K., Gargov, G.: Interval-valued intuitionistic fuzzy sets. Fuzzy Sets Syst. **31**(3), 343–349 (1989)
6. Ye, J.: Prioritized aggregation operators of trapezoidal intuitionistic fuzzy sets and their application to multicriteria decision making. Neural Comput. Appl. **25**(6), 1447–1454 (2014)
7. Govindan, K., Rajendran, S., Sarkis, J., Murugesan, P.: Multi criteria decision making approaches for green supplier evaluation and selection: a literature review. J. Clean. Prod. **98**, 66–83 (2015). https://doi.org/10.1016/j.jclepro.2013.06.046
8. Ayazi, S.A., Moradi, J.S., Paksoy, T.: Supplier selection and order size determination in a supply chain by using fuzzy multiple objective models. J. Multiple-Valued Logic Soft Comput. **23**, 135–160 (2014)
9. Azadnia, A.H., Ghadimi, P., Saman, M.Z.M., Wong, K.Y., Heavey, C.: An integrated approach for sustainable supplier selection using fuzzy logic and fuzzy AHP. Appl. Mech. Mater. **315**, 206–210 (2013)
10. Büyüközkan, G., Çifçi, G.: A novel fuzzy multi-criteria decision framework for sustainable supplier selection with incomplete information. Comput. Ind. **62**, 164–174 (2011). https://doi.org/10.1016/j.compind.2010.10.009
11. Chatterjee, K., Kar, S.: Multi-criteria analysis of supply chain risk management using interval valued fuzzy TOPSIS. OPSEARCH **53**(3), 474–499 (2016). https://doi.org/10.1007/s12597-015-0241-6
12. Smarandache, F.: Neutrosophy/Neutrosophic Probability, Set, and Logic. American Research Press, Rehoboth (1998)
13. Wang, H., Smarandache, F., Zhang, Y.Q., Sunderraman, R.: Single valued neutrosophic sets. Multispace Multistruct. **4**, 410–413 (2010)
14. Ye, J.: Trapezoidal neutrosophic set and its application to multiple attribute decision-making. Neural Comput. Appl. **26**(5), 1157–1166 (2014). https://doi.org/10.1007/s00521-014-1787-6
15. Khatter, K.: Interval Valued Trapezoidal Neutrosophic Set for Prioritization of Non-functional Requirements, arXiv preprint arXiv:1905.05238
16. Khatter, K., Kalia, A.: Quantification of non-functional requirements. In: Sixth International Conference on Contemporary Computing, IC3 2014. pp. 224–229. IEEE computer Society (2014). https://doi.org/10.1109/IC3.2014.6897177

17. Gong, Z., Hai, S.: The interval-valued trapezoidal approximation of interval-valued fuzzy numbers and its application in fuzzy risk analysis. J. Appl. Math. **2014**, 22, Article ID 254853 (2014). https://doi.org/10.1155/2014/254853
18. Atanassov, K.T.: Type-1 fuzzy sets and intuitionistic fuzzy sets. Algorithms **10**(3), 106 (2017)
19. Kim, D.: An integrated supply chain management system: a case study in healthcare sector. In: Bauknecht, K., Pröll, B., Werthner, H. (eds.) EC-Web 2005. LNCS, vol. 3590, pp. 218–227. Springer, Heidelberg (2005). https://doi.org/10.1007/11545163_22

Tweakable Block Mode of Operation for Disk Encompression Using Cipher Text Stealing

Rashmita Padhi$^{(\boxtimes)}$ and B. N. B. Ray

Department of Computer Science and Applications, Utkal University, Vani Vihar,
Bhubaneswar, India

Abstract. In this paper, we study a particular class of symmetric algorithms that aim to ensure confidentiality by using a functionality that is tweakable encipher-ing scheme. A tweakable enciphering scheme is a length preserving encryption protocol which can encrypt messages of varying lengths. The security goal is to satisfy the notion of the tweakable strong pseudorandom permutation (SPRP). Our proposed work is a modified version of XTS that is Xor-Encrypt-Xor with Cipher Text Stealing. This work includes a Galois Field multiplier GF (2^{128}) that can operate in any common field representations. This allows very efficient process-ing of consecutive blocks in a sector. To handle messages whose length is greater than 128-bit but not a multiple of 128-bit.

Keywords: Block cipher · XTS (XOR Encrypt Xor with ciphertext stealing) · Galosis Field multiplier GF (2^{128}) · Strong Pseudorandm Permutation (SPRP) · Tweakable enciphering

1   Introduction

*E*xplosive growth of the digital storage and communication of data require adequate security. Cryptology is the science that aims to provide information security in the digital world. Information security comprises many aspects, the most important of which are confidentiality and authenticity. *Confidentiality* means keeping the information secret from all except those who are authorized to learn or know it. *Authenticity* involves both ensuring that data have not been modified by an unauthorized person (*data integrity*) and being able to verify who is the author of the data (*data origin authentication*). In this paper we provide data encryption with compression by focusing on the tweakable encipher scheme as these appear to offer the best combined security and performance. Our proposed work is a modified version of XTS that is Xor-Encrypt-Xor with Cipher Text Stealing. This work includes a Galois Field multiplier GF (2^{128}) that can operate in any common field representations. This allows very efficient processing of consecutive blocks in a sector. To handle messages whose length is greater than 128-bit but not a multiple of 128-bit. The objective of the work is to develop a fast data encryption system. The requirement is actually to achieve security, speed and error propagation with less consumption of space, i.e., the size of hardware implementation and the amount of secure storage space required.

P. K. Behera and P. C. Sethi (Eds.): CSI 2020, CCIS 1372, pp. 100–108, 2021.
https://doi.org/10.1007/978-981-16-2723-1_11

Data Encryption

Hard disk encryption is usually used to protect all the data on the disk by encrypting it. The whole disk is encrypted with a single/multiple key(s) and encryption/decryption are done on the fly, without user interference. The encryption is on the sector level, that means each sector should be encrypted separately. There are two ways to encrypt a hard disk: at the file level and at the driver level. Encryption at the file level means that every file is encrypted separately. To use a file that's been encrypted, that file must be first decrypted, and then it is used, and then re-encrypts it. Driver-level encryption maintains a logical drive on the user's machine that has all data on it encrypted. In this paper we used AES. The AES is a symmetric block cipher i.e., encryption rule e_k is either the same as decryption rule d_k, or easily derived from it. During one round of AES the entire traffic is divided into fixed block of size 128 bits which is known as a State. AES is an iterated cipher, i.e., ciphers frequently incorporate a sequence of permutation & substitution operations. There are three allowable key lengths, namely 128 bits, 192 bits, and 256 bits. It follows a number of rounds N_r, depends on the key length. $N_r = 10$ if the key length is 128 bits, and $N_r = 12$ if the key length is 192 bits, and $N_r = 14$ if the key length is 256 bits.

2 Existing Work

LRW Mode of Encryption in AES

In LRW mode of AES encryption two keys are used i.e. primary and secondary key. These keys are independent to each other. Each key length is 128 Or 256 bits. In this paper Key_1 and Key_2 are Primary and Secondary keys respectively. The entire message is divided into fixed size blocks which are known as Plain text P. The encryption process is applied to each plaintext block and corresponding cipher text block C is obtained. I is the index of the block.

Input:
P: Fixed size 128 bits Plaintext Block
Key_1: 128 or 256 bits Primary or Cipher Key
Key_2: 128 bits Secondary or Tweak Key
I: Index of data in 128 bit representation
Output:
C: Corresponding Cipher text Block
The following sequence of steps are applied to each plain text block to obtain the Corresponding Cipher text Block :
1. If $I > 2^{128}-1$ or I , exit and output ERROR
2. $T \leftarrow Key_2 \otimes I$
3. $PP \leftarrow P \oplus T$
4. $CC \leftarrow AES\text{-}enc(Key_1, PP)$
5. $C \leftarrow CC \oplus T$
6. Return C

LRW Mode of Decryption in AES

In LRW mode of AES dencryption two keys are used i.e. primary and secondary key. These keys are independent to each other Each key length is 128 0r 256 bits. In this paper Key_1 and Key_2 are Primary and Secondary keys respectively. The decryption process is applied to each Cipher text block C and corresponding Plain text block P is obtained. I is the index of the block.

Input:
C: Fixed size 128 bits Cipher text Block
Key_1: 128 or 256 bits Primary or Cipher Key
Key_2: 128 bits Secondary or Tweak Key
I: Index of data in 128 bit representation
Output:
P: Corresponding Plain text Block
The following sequence of steps are applied to each Cipher text block to obtain the Corresponding Plain text Block :

1. If $I > 2^{128}-1$ or I < Zero
Then exit and Display ERROR as Output
2. $T \leftarrow Key_2 \otimes I$
3. $CC \leftarrow C \oplus T$
4. $PP \leftarrow$ AES-dec (Key_1 ,CC)
5. $C \leftarrow PP \oplus T$
6. return P

Limitations: LRW-AES tweakable mode scope is limited.
    Large volume of data storage cannot be possible using this procedure.

3 Proposed Work

XTS-AES Tweakable Block Cipher
The XTS-AES Tweakable Block Ciphers XEX(Xor-Encrypt-Xor, designed by Rogaway [26])-basd Tweaked Code Book mode (TCB) with Cipher Text Stealing (CTS). Although XEX-TCB-CTS should be abbreviated as XTC, "C" was replaced with "S" (for "stealing") to avoid confusion with the abbreviated ecstasy. Cipher text stealing provides support for sectors with size not divisible by block size, for example, 520-byte sectors and 16-byte blocks.

Meaning of Used Symbols:
Symbols which are used in the equations has the following meaning:

α : Primitive element of Finite Field $GF(2^{128})$
$\oplus$: Bitwise XOR operation
$\otimes$: Two polynomials Multiplication in $GF(2^{128})$
$\leftarrow$: Assigning a value to the variable
$|$: Binary Concatenation
For example , if $N_1 = 1011_2$ and $N_2 = 1110011_2$,
then $N_1 | N_2 = 10111110011_2$.
$\lfloor X \rfloor$: Floor operation of String

Data Units and Tweaks
The size of each data unit must be greater than or equal to 128 bits. The number of blocks having length 128 bits must be less than or equal to $2^{128}-2$. The number of block of size 128-bit should be less than or equal to 2^{20}. A tweak value is assigned to each data unit which is a positive integer. The values of the tweak are assigned sequentially. The assignment of tweak value will be started from any arbitrary positive integer. In AES tweak encryption the tweak will be converted into array of little-endian byte. For example, $123456789A_{16}$ is a tweak value which is converted into byte array $9A_{16}$, 78_{16}, 56_{16}, 34_{16}, 12_{16}.

XEX Tweakable Mode Using Cipher Text Stealing Encryption (XTS-AES Encrypt)
XEX Tweakable Mode using Cipher text Stealing Encryption procedure, a single block of size 128-bit block is implemented by the following equation:

$$C \leftarrow \text{XTS-AES-Encrypt}(Key, P, i, j)$$

Input:
P: Fixed size 128 bits Plain text Block
Key: 512 or 256 bits Cipher Key
i: Tweak value of size 128 bit
j : Sequential number of the data unit

Output:
C: Corresponding Cipher text Block

The key is obtained by concatenating of two fields i. e called Key_1 and Key_2 i.e. Key $= Key_1 | Key_2$. In this case Key_1 and Key_2 are Primary and Secondary keys respectively and both are equal size . The following sequence of steps are perfomed to obtain the corresponding cipher text block .

1) $T \leftarrow \text{AES-enc}(Key_2, i) \otimes \alpha^{Js}$
2) $PP \leftarrow P \oplus T$
3) $CC \leftarrow \text{AES-enc}(Key_1, PP)$
4) $C \leftarrow CC \oplus T$

XTS-AES Encryption of a Data Unit

The encoding process of 128 or more bits plain text block can be implemented by using the following equation:

$$C \leftarrow \text{XTS}text\text{-AES-Encrypt}(Key, P, i)$$

Input:

P: Fixed size 128 bits Plain text Block

Key: 512 or 256 bits Cipher Key

i: Tweak value of size 128 bit

Output:

C: Corresponding Cipher text Block

C is the cipher text which is obtained by using the above operation on the same block size of P. *The entire traffic or message is* partitioned into $m+1$ number of blocks:

$P = P_0 | \ldots P_{m-1} | P_m$

The value of m is the largest integer that is $128m$ P.

The size of the initial m blocks that is $P_0, \ldots, P_{m-1}$ are 128 bits long, and the size of the end block that is Pm is between 0 and 127 bits long. Pm *can be a null string that the size of the string is zero.* The key is obtained by concatenating of two fields i. e called Key_1 and Key_2 i.e. Key = $Key_1 | Key_2$. In this case Key_1 and Key_2 are Primary and Secondary keys respectively and both are equal size . The following sequence of steps are preformed to obtain the corresponding cipher text block .

1)for q ← 0 to m-2 do

a) $Cq \leftarrow$ XTS-AES-Encrypt(Key, P_q, i, q)

2)b ← bit-size of Pm

3)if b=0 then do

a) XTS-AES-Encrypt(Key, P_{m-1}, i, m-1)

b) $C_m \leftarrow$ empty

4)else do

a) CC ← XTS-AES-Encrypt(Key, P_{m-1}, i, m-1)

b) $C_m \leftarrow$ first b bits of CC

c) CP ← last (128-b) bits of CC

d) PP ← P_m | CP

e) $C_{m-1} \leftarrow$ XTS-AES-Encrypt(Key, PP, i, m)

5) $C \leftarrow C_0 | \ldots | C_{m-1} | C_m$

XEX Tweakable Mode Using Cipher Text Stealing Decryption (XTS-AES Decrypt)

XEX Tweakable Mode using Cipher text Stealing Decryption procedure, a single block of size 128-bit block is implemented by the following equation:

$$P \leftarrow \text{XTS}text\text{-AES-Decrypt}(Key, C, i, j)$$

Input:
C: Fixed size 128 bits Cipher text Block
Key: 512 or 256 bits Key
i: Tweak value of size 128 bit
j : Sequential number of the data unit

Output:
P : Corresponding Plain text Block

The key is obtained by concatenating of two fields i.e called Key_1 and Key_2 i.e. Key $= Key_1 | Key_2$. In this case Key_1 and Key_2 are Primary and Secondary keys respectively and both are equal size . The following sequence of steps are perfomed to obtain the corresponding plain text block .

1) $T \leftarrow$ AES-dec (Key_2, i) $\otimes \alpha^{Js}$
2) $CC \leftarrow C \oplus T$
3) $PP \leftarrow$ AES-dec(Key_1, PP)
4) $P \leftarrow PP \oplus T$

XTS-AES Decryption of a Data Unit
The decoding process of 128 or more bits cipher text block can be implemented by using the following equation:

$$P \leftarrow \text{XTS-AES-Decrypt}(Key, C, i)$$

Input:
C: 128 bits Cipher text Block
Key: 512 or 256 bits Cipher Key
i: Tweak value of size 128 bit

Output:
P: Corresponding Plain text Block

P is the plain text which is obtained by using the above operation on the same block size of C. *The entire cipher text is* partitioned into $m+1$ number of blocks:

   $C = C_0 | \ldots | C_{m-1} | C_m$

The value of m is the largest integer that is $128m$ P.
The size of the initial m blocks that is $C_0, \ldots, C_{m-1}$ are 128 bits long, and the size of the end block that is C_m is between 0 and 127 bits long. C_m *can be a null string that the size of the string is zero.* The key is obtained by concatenating of two fields i. e called Key_1 and Key_2 i.e. Key = $Key_1 | Key_2$. In this case Key_1 and Key_2 are Primary and Secondary keys respectively and both are equal size . The following sequence of steps are performed to obtain the corresponding plain text block .

   1) for q ← 0 to m-2 do
       a) Pq ← XTS-AES-Decrypt(Key, Cq, i, q)
   2) b ← bit-size of Cm
   3) if b = 0 then do
a) P_{m-1}← XTS-AES-Decrypt(Key,C_{m-1}, i, m-1)
b) P_m ← empty
   4) else do
a)PP ← XTS-AES-Decrypt(Key, C_{m-1}, i, m)
b)P_m ← first b bits of PP
c) CP ← last (128-b) bits of PP
d)   CC← C_m | CP
e) P_{m-1}← XTS-AES Decrypt(Key, CC, i, m-1)
5. P← $P_0 | \ldots | P_{m-1} | P_m$

4   Performance Analysis

With the wide spread of multi-core processors, speeding up encryption using paralleliza-tion is made possible and parallelization is not a luxury anymore and can increase the performance significantly. Encryption mode of operation should support parallelization. CBC and CFB cannot be parallelized, while XTS can be parallelized on the sector level as each sector is encrypted independently to other sectors. Also a plaintext can be recov-ered from just two adjacent blocks of cipher text. As a consequence, decryption *can* be parallelized.

5 Conclusion

In this paper a highly secure XTS-based Tweaked Block Enciphering scheme with Cipher text Stealing has been proposed for hard disk encryption. The important features of this scheme are the use of Cipher block chaining mode like operations to gain the error propagation property. A one-bit change in a plaintext affects all following cipher text blocks in a sector. The tweak T is calculated by encrypting (using AES) the block address (after being padded with zeros) with the tweak key due to this step the value of the tweak is neither known nor controlled by the attacker. Any difference between two tweaks result full diffusion in both the encryption and decryption directions. All these factors improve security. It has been shown that the proposed mode possesses a high throughput as compression is done before enciphering scheme. Only standard shift and add (xor) operators have been used for the non-linear multiplication function in the finite field $GF(2^{128})$ having $O(1)$ time complexity, therefore gives better resistance against linear cryptanalysis without degradation in performance. This proposed mode has ability to encrypt arbitrary length messages due to the use of cipher text stealing technique.

6 Open Problems

There still remain many open problems in the search for efficient and secure data encryption. It can therefore be hoped that many remaining open problems can be solved in the coming years. These are some of the interesting open problems: that is: There is a lack of good Boolean functions for the tweak generator which are efficient and also resist the cryptanalytic attacks, in particular algebraic and fast algebraic attacks, Extend the current work to audio, and video encryption. The given XEX ciphertext Stealing technique can be efficiently implemented by using AES having key length 256-bit. Introduce the hardware implementation of the entire work.

References

1. Schneier, B.: Applied Cryptography, Second Edn. Wiley Press
2. Stinson, D.R.: Cryptography Theory and Practice, Second Edn. CRC Press
3. Nelson, M., Gailly, J.-L.: The Data Compression Book, Second Edn. M&T Press
4. Sarkar, P.: Efficient Tweakable Enciphering Schemes from (Block-Wise) Universal Hash Functions
5. Chakraborty, D., Sarkar P.: HCH: A New Tweakable Enciphering Scheme Using the Hash-Counter-Hash
6. McGrew, D.: Counter Mode Security: Analysis and Recommendations (2002). https://citeseer.ist.psu.edu/mcgrew02counter.html
7. Rogaway, P., Bellare, M., Black, J.: OCB: A blockcipher mode of operation for efficient authenticated encryption. ACM Trans. Inf. Syst. Secur. 6(3), 365–403 (2003)
8. Schroeppel, R.: The Hasty Pudding Cipher. The first AES conference, NIST (1998). https://www.cs.arizona.edu/~rcs/hpc
9. Liskov, M., Rivest, R.L., Wagner, D.: Tweakable block ciphers. In: Yung, M. (ed.) CRYPTO 2002. LNCS, vol. 2442, pp. 31–46. Springer, Heidelberg (2002). https://doi.org/10.1007/3-540-45708-9_3

10. Goos, G., Hartmanis, J., van Leeuwen, J., Schneier, B. (eds.): FSE 2000. LNCS, vol. 1978. Springer, Heidelberg (2001). https://doi.org/10.1007/3-540-44706-7
11. Fruhwirth, C.: New Methods in Hard Disk Encryption (2005). https://clemens.endorphin.org/nmihde/nmihde-A4-ds.pdf
12. Ferguson, N.: AES-CBC + Elephant diffuser: A Disk Encryption Algorithm for Windows Vista (2006). https://download.microsoft.com/download/0/2/3/0238acaf-d3bf-4a6d-b3d6-0a0be4bbb36e/BitLockerCipher200608.pdf
13. Lempel–Ziv–Welch. https://en.wikipedia.org/wiki/Lempel-Ziv-Welch
14. U.S. Code Collection. https://www4.law.cornell.edu/uscode/35/154.html
15. Blelloch, G.E.: Introduction to Data Compression. https://www.eecs.harvard.edu/~michaelm/CS222/compression.pdf
16. Biham, E., Shamir, A.: Differential cryptanalysis of DES-like cryptosystems. J Cryptol 4(1), 3–72 (1991). https://doi.org/10.1007/BF00630563
17. Matsui, M.: The first experimental cryptanalysis of the data encryption standard. In: Desmedt, Y.G. (ed.) CRYPTO 1994. LNCS, vol. 839, pp. 1–11. Springer, Heidelberg (1994). https://doi.org/10.1007/3-540-48658-5_1
18. Matsui, M.: Linear cryptanalysis method for DES cipher. In: Helleseth, T. (ed.) EUROCRYPT 1993. LNCS, vol. 765, pp. 386–397. Springer, Heidelberg (1994). https://doi.org/10.1007/3-540-48285-7_33

Author Index

Printed in the United States
by Baker & Taylor Publisher Services

Printed in the United States
by Baker & Taylor Publisher Services